ART IN PRACTICE

Motivation and development 3 - 12 years

CRPYK

Margaret Morgan

Nash Pollock
Publishing

In memory of Dick Field and Valerie Thornton,
and for all who value art
in the education of children

© Margaret Morgan 1993

First published 1993

10 9 8 7 6 5 4 3 2

Published by
Nash Pollock Publishing
32 Warwick Street
Oxford OX4 1SX

Orders to:
9 Carlton Close
Grove
Wantage
Oxfordshire OX12 0PU

A catalogue record for this book is available from the British Library

ISBN 1 898255 00 8

Design, typesetting and production by Can Do Design, Buckingham.
Colour origination by Advance Laser Graphic Arts, Hong Kong.
Printed in Hong Kong by Wing King Tong Co. Ltd.

CONTENTS

ACKNOWLEDGEMENTS

Thanks are due to:

The Controller of Her Majesty's Stationery Office for permission to print excerpts from the National Curriculum Art documents for England and Wales; the National Curriculum Council for permission to print excerpts from the Art Non-Statutory Guidance document 1992.

Simon and Schuster for permission to use excerpts from *Art 4 - 11* edited by Margaret Morgan.

Gillian Figg, Principal Lecturer, Primary Education, Swansea Institute of Higher Education for contributing the foreword to this publication.

Michael Chase for permission to use Valerie Thornton's work.

Annetta Hoffnung, Christopher Neve, Andrew Nicholson, Seonaid M. Robertson and Dr Sheila Paine for permission to use quotations.

Deborah Rawson, and South East Arts for permission to use the 'Folk Tales' project, and to the artist Rebecca Price for her contribution in reporting it.

The Greater London Arts Association and the artist Shaheen Mirali for the 'Houses and Homes' project, and to Sue Thomas for writing the report.

David Downes and Simon Whitnall for permission to use their childhood and adult work.

Mark, Bethan Barker, Jessamy Barker, Caroline Doran, Edward Doran, William Doran, Jane Kay, Rachel LeGros, Rachel Petty, Rebecca Turner, Faye Turner and Rebecca Whitnall for permission to use their work.

Dr Gillian Robinson of Anglia Polytechnic University for contributing projects and for her generous support in discussion on the subject of sketchbooks.

Andrew Mutter, Senior Advisory Teacher for Art and Design; Angie Holliday, Drama Advisory Teacher; and the Drama, Dance, Art and Design Teams, Newham Arts Education Centre.

Lynn Gash, Education Officer, and Norwich Castle Museum and Gallery.

Margaret Jackson, for contributing children's work, and for her support in helping to present the manuscript.

Kevin Mathieson and Enfield Teachers' Centre for the section on Computer Art.

John Chataway for assistance with the photography.

The teachers who contributed work, reported or wrote the material for the projects: Madeleine Addyman, Chitra Aloysius, Shaune Amette, Jo Barnard, Wendy Benest, Tina Brown, Juliet Croydon, Kathryn Elcoat, Julia Holland, Jane Homes, Sheila Manners, Joanne Masters, Carole Moran, Gwenda Smale, Janet Swann, Ann Taylor, Carrie Taylor, Valerie Turner, and Tim Wilson (Advisory Art and Design Teacher, Suffolk).

Ray Petty, Art and Design Adviser for Suffolk, for his contribution in planning, discussion and support; Norman Manners, General Adviser, Art and Design, for Norfolk (until 1993); Julia Page, Art Adviser for the London Borough of Enfield; and Carol Radcliffe, Senior Inspector for the London Borough of Newham, for their interest and support.

The headteachers, staff and children of the following schools: Beckton Special School, London Borough of Newham; Beccles Middle School, Suffolk; Beyton Middle School, Suffolk; Belstead Special School, Ipswich, Suffolk; Broomsgrove County Junior School, Wivenhoe, Essex; Eversley Infants School, London Borough of Essex; Grange Primary School, Felixstowe, Suffolk; Holland Park County Primary School, Clacton, Essex; Ixworth Middle School, Suffolk; Northfields First School, Norwich, Norfolk; Parlaunt Park Combined School, Slough, Berkshire; Prince of Wales Primary School, Enfield; Redgrave and Botesdale School, Suffolk; St Andrew's First and Middle School, Cobham, Surrey; St Helen's Primary School, Brentwood, Essex; Suffolks Primary School, London Borough of Enfield; The Sarah Bonnell School, London Borough of Newham; The Latymer School, London Borough of Enfield; West Lea Special School, Enfield; Whitton Primary School, Ipswich, Suffolk; Winchmore Junior School, London Borough of Enfield.

Sincere apologies to any persons who have been inadvertently omitted from the list, or who have not been traceable.

FOREWORD

It is heartening in the current climate to come across a book like this which is neither threatened by the National Curriculum nor driven by it. Rather, it is a consideration of how children respond to the good practice of their teachers. Margaret Morgan describes it as being a book that comes 'from the inside out' - and I know exactly what she means: we are given case studies of work done by real children in real contexts. The book then draws back from the nitty-gritty and detail of actual classroom projects to analyse their relationships to the National Curriculum orders.

In my opinion, it is the best way to tackle the National Curriculum. As a member of the former Art Working Group, I was always conscious that, because of the subject-led structure of the orders, it was not within our remit to be explicit about how the knowledge, skills and understanding specific to art related directly to the nature of the developing child. Yet it is an understanding of the relationship between the nature of the subject and the nature of the child that lies at the heart of good teaching. The eternal dilemma for the teacher is when, and how, to intervene. Indeed, the National Curriculum was established in part as a reaction to the non-interventionist philosophies practised by some in the fifties and sixties. Teachers were aware that the prescriptive methods practised previously did not allow for children's individual creativity and expression to develop - but, unfortunately, neither did complete non-intervention by the teacher. A framework, a structure, is needed in order to set children free to grow and it is the teacher who provides this, albeit within the context of the National Curriculum.

In this book we see how individual teachers can choose to interpret the orders. It uses exemplar material, not only of individual children's work, but also collaborative group and class projects. Interestingly, it looks at good practice both at home and in school and bites the bullet of assessment, monitoring and evaluation, addressing it in an accessible and 'user friendly' way. In short, it is a comprehensive account of all the things primary teachers need to be thinking about. I will be recommending it to my student teachers, and to all the teachers I meet in the course of my work. I will tell them that it is a practical guide to primary art teaching that has children at its heart, and that is supported by an appropriate leavening of sound philosophy. It helps to flesh out and humanises the National Curriculum orders.

Margaret Morgan is an example of the very best kind of adviser/consultant: one who has always been able to inspire teachers to achieve the best practice, by valuing their work and by helping them to share it with others. By persuading them to document it clearly and attractively in this publication, Margaret Morgan's influence on children and teachers can extend far beyond only those with whom she has had personal contact.

Gillian Figg
Principal Lecturer, Primary Education
Swansea Institute of Higher Education

Member of former National Curriculum Art Working Group

Looking at onions. Cut paper. 11 years. 37 x 30 cm

1 INTRODUCTION

This book has been written in the belief that Art is of vital importance to our children and their education.

It is a subject discipline in its own right and, like a primary colour, nothing else can stand in its stead, although it can be a key component in some interesting and valuable mixtures.

It is sometimes helpful to make sure we are aware of the two major strands in this whole experience. First, the *expressive*, which links art with the other arts, giving opportunity for a variety of human expression, and interrelating naturally when the idea requires; second, the *design* aspect, which links it with curriculum areas concerned with planning, crafting and making, and evaluation processes and activities.

Art and design experience in an educational context is essentially practical, making use of the clear logic of visual and tactile language, while also taking into account the intuitive modes of approach. This practice is interrelated with, and supported by, a component of critical studies - response to, and understanding of the made forms of the world past and present. At the heart of this experience lies the discovery of how materials are reshaped and reformed to make statements of personal expression, or to fulfil perceived needs in the context of environmental design and the production of functional objects. Art and design can be seen as a powerful contributor to other curriculum areas, in particular to Design and Technology, but also to Humanities, Language, Mathematics, Science, Music and P.E.

The potential of learning based on art and design experience can be developed in many ways, but in particular in

- its function as a natural visual language of communication
- its use as an analytical tool to record the visual world
- exploration of language and image links
- the translation of the visual world into elements appropriate for designing
- solving problems and helping to clarify the sequences of processes involved.

It is only when we consider the potential of the children we teach and the nature of art and design in the context of a soundly structured developmental programme, that we can begin to enjoy the positive aspects of what this wonderful discipline has to offer. I have chosen to approach the matter through children's practical work and understanding, supported by examples of what I believe to be sound and positive teaching methods.

In the first place it will be necessary to consider the value, nature and importance of art, craft and design education for children between the ages of three and twelve years. The main philosophy is based in a deep respect for the child's own thinking and contribution, which in turn relies on the teacher's skills in diagnosing the stage reached, and enabling further developments to take place.

The work included in the book comes from children of all stages of development and ability, including those with special educational needs. The main emphasis is on the demonstration of good practice undertaken in school and at home. I have selected work which shows enthusiasm, involvement, vigour, inventiveness, skill and learning and is the outcome of children being enabled to think and act for themselves. Whatever experience the children have had prior to coming to school, or working with a particular teacher, their understanding, performance and self reward can be much enhanced by appropriate teaching and support. To be of any real value this will need to be grounded on a challenging developmental curriculum, appropriately stimulating environment, and good quality basic tools, materials and resources.

Clearly process is as important as end product, as it is only in understanding the ways in which children are thinking and working that we - and they - can assess what is happening, where the strengths, weaknesses and present and future developments may lie.

It is significant that research has shown that the two hemispheres of the brain undertake different functions, *verbal analytical processing* being undertaken by the left hemisphere, encompassing sequential, symbolic, linear and objective experience, and *spatial global processing* pertaining to the right, with its intuitive, selective, relational, time-free mode of operation.

With appropriate cross-linking, which is built into the brain mechanism, these two aspects can be seen to embody a wonderful tool enabling us to function effectively in a challenging world. It is of the utmost importance that we see the rational and intuitive modes of response in balance if children are to develop to their full potential.

In the past the bias was heavily weighted toward the verbal analytical approach. It was surely a misunderstanding to think that a well-educated person was one who could translate everything into words, or could work out all the challenges life throws at us through them. Of course words are important, but we need to think for a moment of the part that intuition plays in our response to everyday living, to convince ourselves of the necessity of balance. Understanding that creative and intuitive problem-solving, making sense of experience, and leaps of insight are as relevant to the scientist and designer as to the artist or musician, enables us to see the importance of nonverbal and preverbal aspects of our children's education. Betty Edwards speaks of the 'Ah-ha' response - the 'I've got it!' - 'I see the picture!'

Experience in art is based on feeling and analytical responses which can be enhanced and illuminated by verbal means, but which by their very nature do not depend on them, and cannot be totally described by them.

The practice of art is such a fundamental one that it would be inappropriate in the first place to think of it from any limited departure or point of view, be they present trends, personal theories, or particular curricula. These are the means by which we harness the reality to what we believe to be good educational practice, but we must never lose sight of the nature of the reality itself. We are in fact dealing with a whole body of knowledge which human beings have been involved in ever since they developed the means to respond to causes by means of understanding effects, and by using the resources of this planet to make and use things which fulfilled their needs - be they practical or spiritual.

The initial experiences from which our responses grow are 'processed' in a variety of ways and are based on sensory learning with an emphasis on sight and touch. Children's ability to develop this all-important sensitivity can be enhanced by good teaching and is as important throughout the stages of learning as it is initially.

Sensory learning is assimilated and acted upon by rational and intuitive means and therefore involves thinking as well as feeling, in fact involving us as whole people.

Many primary teachers and educationists have seen in art and design education at its best, the embodiment of a way of responding, knowing and acting which is unique in its own right. It is not surpising that they have rejected simplistic teacher-directed picture and model making for more valuable and challenging approaches which really change the way in which children face the world of learning.

An essential quality of humanity is the need to find out about the nature and potential of materials. Even the youngest children seem to have an inbuilt urge to involve themselves in the physical act of handling - pushing, pulling, squeezing, building, destroying - then going through the whole process again. We have only to watch children as they are deeply involved in (so-called) play activities with sand, clay, porridge, jam, bricks, wood, straw, twigs, fabric, or any other materials to realise that they are building up their experience of the nature of the substance and its potential. This in fact is no different to the needs in adult life of designers, architects or craftspeople who must understand the qualities of the media and materials they use in order to design or make successfully. It is in doing that we so often learn, as much if not more than in learning about things in theory that we are enabled to 'do'. The key words for much of our learning experience throughout life could be based on *sensitivity - exploration - using - sensitivity -* which should be seen in continuous cyclic form rather than in a linear way.

To enable children to come to positive terms with the experiences of investigating, making, knowing and understanding are powerful and reasonable requirements for any curriculum.

Robots pretending to fight.
Boy, 4 years. 25 x 31 cm

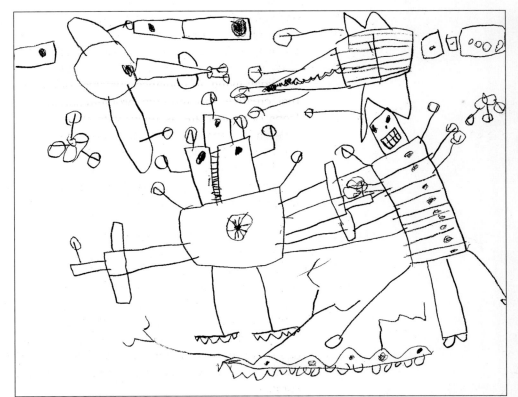

2 THE NATIONAL CURRICULUM

This book has not been planned as a full comprehensive course, but aims to show good teaching and practice through presenting children's work done individually, in groups and in whole classes.

A broad range of practice has been included, and each project can be considered and weighed against the appropriate level of criteria.

In a world of changing values and new initiatives in education it is of the greatest importance that we appraise and evaluate our own practice in art, craft and design in the context of the needs of the children we teach, the school we work in, and the demands of statutory requirements relevant to us.

In particular for those of us who come under the aegis of the National Curriculum for England and Wales we shall be dealing with the work of children leading to and including Key Stages 1 and 2, and overlapping into the first year of Key Stage 3.

In England this curriculum is divided into two sections under the headings of

Attainment Target 1   -   Investigating and Making

Attainment Target 2   -   Knowledge and Understanding.

In Wales there are three sections:

Attainment Target 1   -   Understanding

Attainment Target 2   -   Making

Attainment Target 3   -   Investigating.

These components when seen as a breakdown of the whole experience of art, craft and design offer a wonderfully comprehensive sphere to work in. Perhaps when seen in this light, as a whole, the content falls into a natural context.

The Non-Statutory Guidance firmly states that the Attainment Targets require 'an integrated approach to teaching' and 'constantly intertwine in all art lessons' (England), and 'The activities should be interwoven so that the learning derived from each serves to reinforce learning in the others' (Wales). In England the two components are in fact weighted 2 to 1 in the order printed. It contains no new message or philosophy of art education, but for some teachers the concept of linking children's understanding of the work of artists and designers to children's practical activity may need to be developed to a deeper and more structured level.

Whatever the situation, in the first place it is useful to consider the practice in our own school as it stands at the present time, and to take a cool and thoughtful look from the 'inside-out', as well as from the 'outside-in'; in other words, to look at the responses and work of our particular children in relation to the curriculum as it stands, before considering the implications of any statutory requirements. It is crucial that existing energy and good practice on the part of teachers and children is not lost in the implementation of any new curriculum venture. In relation to these particular requirements they need not be.

The main requirement is for a broad, balanced developmental programme of learning which pays due attention to understanding and work which has been undertaken before. It requires children to have experience which includes work in three dimensions as well as two, and in a variety of scales - as individuals, groups and whole classes.

It requires them to be able to make appropriate use of information and to evaluate their own work, and that of others.

It includes an area of experience and response leading to understanding and appreciation of art in a variety of modes and styles from a variety of cultures, past and present, Western and worldwide.

On looking at this overall package many teachers will recognise their own and their children's current practice. Others may find aspects which are lightweight or even missing altogether, and this will mean that some challenging developments need to be undertaken. It is important that children learn - to think for themselves, explore, experiment, control and use, in response to challenge, and for their own needs and purposes. They should be encouraged to communicate and express ideas, and to handle materials and tools over as wide a range of challenges as they are likely to meet in this incredibly diverse world of ever changing life patterns.

The crux of the matter lies in the attitudes we foster, and our insights into the way in which the child works - how involved, inventive, creative, determined and skilled he or she has been. Is there evidence of development? Does one thing lead to another? Does the child demonstrate particular abilities in his or her work, or in talking about it? These aspects are as much if not more important than the end product; in fact the end product, educationally speaking, does not exist other than in its rightful place in the sequence of thinking, experimentation, appraisal and statement - whichever order they may occur in. At whatever point we meet a child it is the teacher's skill in diagnosing the stage reached which will set the course for further development and learning.

Girl, 7 years.
Museum study: Mask.
19 x 15 cm

There is a central body of experience in art and design curriculum which undergirds sensory learning of all kinds. It calls for a strong basis of direct experience and emphasises the importance of children 'looking at' things and 'talking about' them and their own work. The developmental nature of the curriculum is made quite clear as it unfolds, and it is possible to see the differing requirements which should be understood as steps on which to build all kinds of relevant and exciting experience.

It is quite useful to select key words from the National Curriculum for both England and Wales in order to clarify the nature of these steps. They are so similar in approach and general philosophy, and overlap to such an extent that it is useful to put them in one list.

Up to the age of 7 years (Key Stage 1) the children's activities are grounded on *investigating, making, knowing, understanding, observing, remembering, imagining, recording, exploring, talking about, describing, responding, collecting, selecting, sorting, recreating, organising, modifying, recognising, identifying* and the splendidly realistic *beginning to make connections,* or *beginning to compare.*

These are all beautifully ongoing descriptions of activities, without beginning or end - the kind of words which must surely lie at the very foundations of good primary education, and although they are seen here in the context of art and design, they are also relevant to the disciplines of language, science, humanities, technology and mathematics.

In Key Stage 2 all the experience of the earlier years is subsumed and continually developed. It goes on quite naturally, and builds up into a second list: *representing, communicating ideas and feelings, developing ideas or themes, working collaboratively, experimenting, applying knowledge, planning and making, using a variety of methods, choosing appropriate media, adapting and modifying, refining, identifying different kinds of art, comparing, looking for... characteristics... purposes, discussing.*

In this list a highly personal thinking, feeling response is being fostered, together with steady build-up of skills and control. This, together with the ever broadening experience of art and design forms past and present, from all kinds of cultures, should offer a sound foundation for the 12-year-old to begin to build the next phase, hopefully with interest, enjoyment and confidence.

It is useful to note that at all levels in any kind of assessment judgements are to be made on 'accumulated evidence' (see Chapter 3). Children as well as teachers should be able to see their own work in sequence over a period of practice, so that they can begin to understand, assess and monitor their own potential strengths and weaknesses.

In Key Stage 2 sketchbooks are compulsory - every child must have one and be enabled to use it. (See Chapter 5, Sketchbooks.)

The emphasis in Key Stage 3 is on the child's independent practice and initiative, making use of the still ongoing development of skills and attitudes fostered in the earlier years: *using expressive and technical skills, developing and sustaining chosen ideas or themes, applying a broad understanding of the elements of art, modifying and explaining, identifying and demonstrating knowledge and understanding, imaginatively applying methods and approaches, analysing, evaluating, examining.*

Any sound curriculum should enable every child to hold the key to understanding and enjoying art and design not only in a school context, but as a positive experience which can be built on later in life. It is worth asking ourselves whether in fact we do enable this when we begin to appraise our own work as teachers.

It will always be necessary to plan the structured curriculum in a way which allows for initiative and immediate enthusiasms to flourish. The Non-Statutory Guidance is supportive on this point, stating ' ... That within the specific Programmes of Study ... there should be sufficient flexibility for teachers and

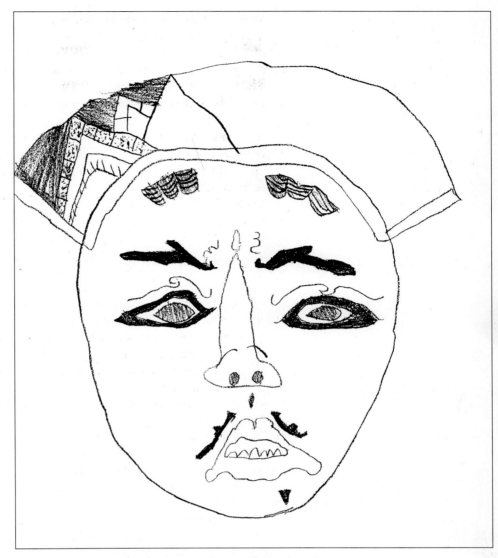

Boy, 7 years. Museum study: Mask. 27 x 20 cm

pupils to follow their particular interests.' This curriculum is no straightjacket unless we interpret it as such.

Depending on how we understand, assimilate and use the National Curriculum in art and design, it can be seen as either a negative and restrictive force or a very useful vehicle in which to travel to some interesting destinations. The choice is our own.

3 ASSESSMENT, MONITORING AND EVALUATION

Assessment, monitoring and evaluation are part and parcel of the teaching process. It is only when they are viewed as appendages that real difficulties arise, and the value of the process can be lost or seriously diminished.

If assessment is seen as a valuable tool for the teacher to use to understand the quality of the child's thinking and acting, it becomes clear that what is said or reported by way of assessment should be of prime teaching effectiveness. In this structure there should be no place for any paraphernalia of unwieldy if well intentioned requirements, tick lists or screeds of record notes. What is not of practical value to the education of the individual, and to those who teach him or her, has no place.

The statutory nature of the National Curriculum requirements sharpen our thinking about the assessment of performance, which has to be considered very carefully as a whole-school policy. Each member of staff must be quite clear about the aims, objectives, and the agreed means of carrying them out. The means (which the National Curriculum does not specify) is a challenge for each school to plan, and a strategy which undergirds the main purpose of the whole exercise is needed. It must ensure and show evidence of continuous and well grounded development in the child as he or she moves through the education system from teacher to teacher or from school to school.

Assessing performance is an appropriate and reasonable requirement as well as a positive and powerful force when well handled. To work effectively teachers and children need to understand the purpose of the process, and the nature and significance of the criteria on which any judgements are made. For a child's work and performance to be considered on criteria which have bever been introduced and discussed, is like putting up goal posts in (from the children's point of view) rather surprising places after the game is over.

The recommendations in the National Curriculum Non-Statutory Guidance section state firmly that the system should be *flexible, manageable* and *straight-forward*, and it follows that *'assessment should be simple for teachers and pupils'*.

Record keeping should be kept to a minimum, and be made up of material which really does give appropriate information to enlighten the present and enable future teaching decisions.

ASSESSMENT: THE THREE BASICS

To state the obvious, there are three basics: *The Child, The Teacher* and *The Work*. The order in which they should be considered is arguable, and it is difficult to look at any one in isolation without noting the interrelationship of a number of factors.

The Child

The target of the teaching - a thinking, feeling human being whose performance is to be assessed and monitored. To be seen in turn as *maker, assessor, monitor* and *evaluator* of his or her own approach and work.

1 As maker - responding to challenges, inner drives, and working in a number of different modes, materials and techniques in two and three dimensions.

in their own right, which must make sense if read without the supporting evidence, but which could not be proven without it.

Many teachers will find that looking at work from previous years is far more informative than reading records by colleagues who are perhaps not as experienced in assessing art and design work, or whose values are different, or whose judgements may be idiosyncratic. While the success of a sound overall school policy is the aim, it will take time before all members of staff feel confident to make appropriate judgements in this curriculum area. It is the work, seen in sequence, which shows what really has been happening.

National Curriculum assessment is based on the end of Key Stage statements. In the documents they appear under separate headings - 'Investigating and Making' and 'Knowledge and Understanding' (England) - and 'Understanding', 'Making', and 'Investigating' (Wales) but here I have chosen to present them in one list (see pp 18-19). This is to make the point of the assessment covering the whole art and design spectrum. It would be quite possible for a single piece, or sequence of work to be judged from a number of different criteria, covering more than one heading.

RECORD KEEPING

This is an area in which there must be an overall school policy, and in which teachers need a highly disciplined approach. The *minimum of clearly communicated information should be presented* - which will enable reasonable monitoring and tracking of the child's progress. It must be easily understandable for teachers other than the record-keeper, parents and children (the very young excepted of course). There can be no place here for one-word contributions of the nature of 'good' 'satisfactory' 'weak' and the like. The record should describe the positive aspects of understanding and practice, and the problems raised and tackled. The yardstick must always be whether the writer, if she was to receive it, would herself find the record clear enough to understand, with implications for future teaching needs.

The record, together with the evidence of the folder, should be a sound base from which to consider future developments.

ENGLAND

KEY STAGE 1

By the end of Key Stage 1 pupils should be able to:

AT1: Investigating and making

a represent in visual form what they observe, remember and imagine.

b select from a range of items they have collected and use them as a basis for their work.

c work practically and imaginatively with a variety of materials and methods exploring the elements of art.

d implement simple changes in their work in the light of progress made.

AT2: Knowledge and understanding

a recognise different kinds of art.

b identify some of the ways in which art has changed, distinguishing between work in the past and present.

c begin to make connections between their own work and that of other artists

KEY STAGE 2

By the end of Key Stage 2 pupils should be able to:

AT1: Investigating and making

a communicate ideas and feelings in visual form based on what they observe, remember and imagine.

b develop an idea or theme for their work, drawing on visual and other sources, and discuss their methods.

c experiment with, and apply their knowledge of, the elements of art, choosing appropriate media.

d modify their work in the light of its development and their original intentions.

AT2: Knowledge and understanding

a identify different kinds of art and their purposes.

b begin to identify the characteristics of art in a variety of genres from different periods, cultures and traditions, showing some knowledge of the related historical background.

c make imaginative use in their own work of a developing knowledge of the work of other artists.

KEY STAGE 3

By the end of Key Stage 3 pupils should be able to:

AT1: Investigating and making

a Use expressive and technical skills to analyse and present in visual form what they observe, remember and imagine.

b Develop and sustain a chosen idea or theme in their work, investigating and explaining their use of a range of visual and other sources.

c Apply a broad understanding of the elements of art and the characteristics of materials, tools and techniques to implement their ideas.

d Modify their work as it progresses, reviewing its development and meaning, and explain the reasons for change.

AT2: Knowledge and understanding

a Identify the conventions used by artists and assess critically their effect.

b Demonstrate a knowledge and understanding of the principal features of our artistic heritage and appreciate a variety of other artistic traditions.

c Apply imaginatively the methods and approaches of other artists in the presentation of their own ideas and feelings.

KEY STAGE 1

By the end of Key Stage 1 pupils should be able to:

AT1: Understanding

a begin to make connections between their own work and that of others, including artists, craftworkers and designers;

b recognise and begin to compare various kinds of art, craft and design, and their purposes.

AT2: Making

a explore basic aspects of the visual language of art, craft and design;

b work practically and imaginatively with a range of materials and tools;

c make changes to their work as it progresses.

AT3: Investigating

a record images, ideas and feelings from direct observation, memory, and the imagination;

b use a range of items they have collected and organised as a basis for their work and talk about what they have done.

KEY STAGE 2

By the end of Key Stage 2 pupils should be able to:

AT1: Understanding

a make imaginative use of a developing knowledge and understanding of the work of other artists, craftworkers and designers;

b recognise how the works of artists, craftworkers and designers are influenced by different cultures, contexts and times.

AT2: Making

a apply a basic understanding of the visual language of art, craft and design to achieve a variety of technical and expressive outcomes using a range of materials and tools;

b review and modify their work in the light of their intentions.

AT3: Investigating

a select and record images, ideas and feelings from direct observation, memory and imagination, using a range of materials and methods;

b prepare and develop an idea or theme for their work by collecting and organising visual and other resources; discuss their methods.

KEY STAGE 3

By the end of Key Stage 3 pupils should be able to:

AT1: Understanding

a use imaginatively in the development and the presentation of their ideas and feelings an understanding of some of the methods and approaches employed by other artists, craftworkers and designers;

b compare, contrast and evaluate the work of artists, craftworkers and designers and recognise that images, symbols and objects are influenced by diverse cultural and social conventions.

AT2: Making

a apply a broad knowledge of the visual language of art, craft and design; experiment with a range of media and use appropriate materials, tools and techniques in the implementation of their ideas;

b modify their work as it progresses, reviewing its development and meaning in the light of initial ideas.

AT3: Investigating

a use a variety of methods to record and present their observations, feelings and ideas working from direct experience, memory and the imagination;

b develop a chosen idea or theme by exploring a range of visual and other sources; discuss the method and result of their investigation.

4 CHILDREN'S NEEDS

Sun, trees, Mummy, Daddy,
Susan, William, Abby.
Boy, 3 years. 24 x 58 cm

In order to structure effective educational practice it is necessary to look very carefully at the children we are responsible for and to try to understand the nature of their motivation, thinking and action. Good primary teaching has always taken into account the child in the 'here and now', his or her potential, and presentation of appropriate challenge at the right time. All of us put up barriers if we do not know, but feel that we should, and learning processes can degenerate from the moment that we are inwardly cut off from real understanding. Can any of us say that there are never times when we do not move into a defensive game which lets us look as if we know what is going on, whereas in reality we play for time? We learn to cover if for some reason we are afraid, or deem it inappropriate to ask questions. In a situation such as this, children respond in many ways, ranging from making every effort to appear inconspicuous to the teacher's eye, to quite extreme behaviour patterns. No human being finds it easy to cope with feelings of inadequacy.

It requires skill on the part of the teacher to see the point children have really reached, and to give them a security which never makes them lose face when they ask questions, however inappropriate they may at times seem. The main aim must be to find the best means for harnessing potential and personal energies in order to educate. In our quest for understanding the ways in which pupils are thinking in terms of art and design, we would be bypassing a very significant tool in arriving at the point of development reached if we did not take into consideration the development of children's imagery, basing our findings on the evidence of the actual work. The authors of the publication *Art 4-11* (edited by Margaret Morgan) took into consideration various theories of development, their significance and interpretation, together with their own teaching experience.

They state that in spite of the dangers any generalised sequence might have if all children were to be identified simplistically in its context, they believe it to be a useful tool in assisting in understanding. They go on to define five modes of working, pointing out the fact that children move from one to another as appropriate for the task in hand, or at will.

Looking at children's art - a general pattern of sequential development

1 **Experimentation and experience of materials and tools** (← 18 months - 18 years →)

2 **Symbolic interpretation**. In the early years (← 3 - 7/8 years →) this will be based on holistic scanning and global vision. It can continue into adult years as a valid option for communication and expression.

3 **Predominantly symbolist approach**. At this stage (← 5 - 12 years→) the child will be showing a growing interest in a variety of items and a complexity of images; there will be evidence of a visual analytic approach in parts of the work.

4 **Predominantly analytic approach** (← 7/8 years→ onwards). In this mode, the need for visual realism is paramount. Matching and comparisons are important, but symbolist overtones will often be apparent.

5 **Analytic approach** (← 7/8 years→ onwards). This mode is characterised by visual realism based on personal experience through the senses and interpreted through the use of a variety of media.

When we look carefully at children's work, the criteria we as teachers bring to bear must depend on the stage reached, or the mode in which the child is working. For example, to look at a symbolic drawing and make value judgements on it from a solely analytic standpoint would not only be a waste of time, but confusing and damaging to the child.

Whatever the age and stage the children have reached when first we meet them, they will have had a lot of sensory and practical experience from babyhood onward, with all the thinking and trying to make sense of their world which goes on ceaselessly. There will of course be many external influences, not least from their interaction (or deprivation) in regard to adults or other members of the family. It will of course always be important to build up sensory experience systematically in school and outside, and I shall be returning to this subject; but in the first place it is important to look at the way in which the children are thinking, and the conclusions they may have come to, because these are the bases on which they will build whatever we offer them educationally. Sometimes when we find out what is going on we understand some of the confusions which may have arisen in their minds or our own. The preconceptions children carry can be astounding (not only in the context of art) and it can be illuminating to talk to them about what they think art is even when they are very young. This can be undertaken in the first place in a simple and natural way.

Here are some examples of the way in which children have answered these questions about what art is: 'drawing', 'drawing and painting', 'drawing, painting and modelling', 'making things', 'painting with feelings', 'drawing and painting things to look real', 'drawing things right', 'painting with the right colours', 'when people paint with nice colours', 'when you can draw people, and you can tell who it is - like a photograph' ...

In order to extend children's expectation and experience, and to enable them to understand that there are many valid ways of making art, we can introduce all kinds of art and design forms. Ideally originals should be used, but these will need to be augmented by reproductions. We can also introduce pictures in relation to stories - in the form of book illustrations, or in the context of language development, history, or any other curriculum aspect as well as art. Since the aim is initially to find out something of the child's preconceptions and criteria for making judgements as well as adding to experience, the first question may well be 'What do you think about this?' The second question, the important one, is 'Why do you say that?'

Of the many examples which could be given, the following may offer insight into the potential of this approach.

1 Six-year-old Ann looking at a Picasso painting, 'Woman and Doves'.

Ann   'It's lovely.'

Teacher   'Tell me why.'

Ann   'It has lovely colours, and I like that shape.' (pointing to one of the circular shapes the artist had used to depict the woman's breasts)

Teacher   'What is the picture about?'

Ann   'Just lovely colours and birds and things.'

She did not in fact identify the human figure, but could enjoy the painting for the aesthetic qualities of colour and shape.

2 Eight-year-old Claire looking at the Picasso 'Weeping Woman'.

Claire   'Why did he paint like that?'

Teacher   'Do you think he was trying to paint a likeness of someone?'

Claire   'No, I don't think he was.'

Teacher   'What else could it be?'

Claire   'He could have been trying to put how she was feeling... it's sort of how I feel if I get angry and cry.'

Many teachers who respect children's thinking will know that when enthusiasm runs high it is possible for them to defy all limitations of apparent ability or technique and make great leaps forward in performance and understanding. Effective teachers are very often not so much self imposers as creative listeners and watchers who can sensitively introduce new challenges which extend the children's experience at the right time. This in no way negates the need for an overall structured curriculum model which the teacher can use as a skeletal structure; but the model becomes from the outset what it ought to be - bare bones which require to be fleshed out and brought to life by the dynamic of life and spirit.

The whole attitude of awareness and sensitivity is the very lifeblood of creative work, and one which we would do well to foster in a number of different contexts, including the challenges of human interaction and relationships.

SENSORY LEARNING

The fundamental need for each child to be enabled to learn through the senses is a prerequisite not only for art and design, but also for cross-curricular educational practice of all kinds. It is interesting that at times it is so much a part of the hidden curriculum that it is not externalised and structured as an underlying ground base on which personal experience can grow. We need every part of our sensory make-up to function keenly if we are to use our true potential. This is as relevant to children who have full use of all their faculties as for those who are physically impaired, or have learning difficulties where compensatory factors will be critical.

It is possible for all of us to listen and not hear, to look and not see. Sensory learning will need to be encouraged and systematically built up in the context of whatever experience we are involved in. John Fulton in his book *Materials in Design and Technology* speaks of 'naturally motivated beginnings enriched by responsive support and informed teaching', which soundly underlines one of the most effective modes of teaching on which later challenge can be built. However far children may develop, this method is effective and relevant.

In order to foster sensory learning children will need to be surrounded by as much 'reality' and interest as we can muster in our schools, and outside.

As teachers, practical consideration of the school and classroom environment, selecting and presenting stimuli, tools and materials, seeing that they are well organised and cared for, should be seen for what it is - overt teaching. Without basic materials and tools the richness and range of potential cannot be experienced.

Basic materials
Clays and other malleable materials
Wood in solid and sheet format
Textiles - sheet, threads and fibres
Papers, and other sheet materials
Pigment - paints and dyes
Composites, or plastics where appropriate and available

In the final analysis, the importance of each child being helped toward the realisation that they are responsible for their own decisions and actions, and that there are a number of ways of approaching any problem, cannot be underestimated. In this respect, the child has very definite needs which we as teachers will be at pains to fulfil. They are about the build up of motivation, confidence, the ability to research, perseverance, skill and understanding.

The strength of primary education lies in the fact that it is so firmly and organically rooted in the needs of children, and the curriculum must be interpreted as an enabling rather than a thwarting agent.

Robin Tanner, teacher, Her Majesty's Inspector and artist, in conversation about teaching once said 'I really don't *do* anything - I only try to introduce people to themselves.'

It is when we are most at one with ourselves, and secure and confident in the acceptance of our own thinking, that our most effective performance can take place.

Criteria for success

Finally, in addressing children's needs we must above all consider the content of the curriculum we offer them. In the National Curriculum Council's Non-Statutory Guidance the section entitled 'Criteria for Success' very simply lists what they believe children should be able to do. It is an excellent tool for making judgements on curricular practice.

CRITERIA FOR SUCCESS
KEY STAGE 1
AT 1
Pupils should demonstrate that they can:

- start to look closely at the natural and made world and to record what they see;
- be confident in using their memories and imaginations in developing their ideas for art;
- be willing to explore the use of a variety of materials, tools and resources for practical work;
- understand that art has its own language, lines, shapes, colours, etc. and show some awareness of this in their work;
- control tools safely, organise and care for materials and equipment;
- develop the practice of planning their work: try out ideas beforehand, be prepared to change parts if needed.

AT 2
Pupils should demonstrate that they can:

- look closely at artefacts and objects (including their own work) and talk about them with others;

- start to understand that ideas and feelings can be expressed and communicated through art;
- understand that there are connections between their own and others' work, and the work of artists past and present.

KEY STAGE 2
AT 1

Pupils should demonstrate that they can:

- select aspects of the natural and made world and record what they see, imagine and feel;
- take some responsibility for gathering information in support of their work and be discriminating in using it;
- be selective in their choice and application of materials to suit the task;
- develop control, confidence and understanding in using different materials and techniques;
- experiment with the elements of art and begin to use more formal ways to communicate ideas and feeling, e.g. scale, distortion;
- be able to visualise ideas, discuss them with others and modify them with justification.

AT 2

Pupils should demonstrate that they can:

- discuss the different purposes of art and describe how artists have represented their ideas, making use of an art vocabulary;
- recognise and discuss the work of a number of artists, representing different styles and periods, and understand something of the times in which their work was made and how their work influenced others;
- apply what they have learned from other artists' work in an imaginative way to inform their own.

KEY STAGE 3
AT 1

Pupils should demonstrate that they can:

- analyse the appearance, structure and function of what they see and record their observations and ideas for different purposes;
- collect, analyse and organise relevant information to develop their own thinking, imagination and ideas;
- systematically explore the qualities of different media;
- use a wide range of media with confidence and understanding, showing efficiency in organising and completing the task;
- interpret formal codes and conventions in making a personal response;
- take account of their own and others' evaluations in the planning, development and completion of their work.

AT 2

Pupils should demonstrate that they can:

- analyse the different ways artists use to convey meaning;
- express and justify opinions about art;
- understand the key features of major styles and periods in art history and realise how particular artists contributed both to these and to the development of art;
- use what they have learned from other artists' work to guide and enhance their own thinking and practical work.

5 SKETCHBOOKS

EXPLORATION,
experimentation,
searching,
researching,
recording,
celebrating

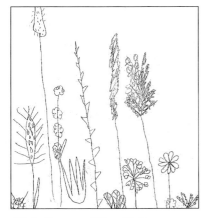

Girl, 6 years. 21 x 18.5 cm

*Inside outside. Girl, 9 years.
23 x 25.5 cm*

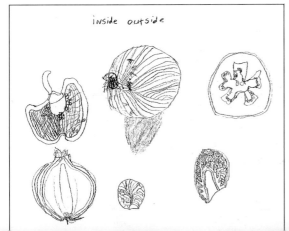

The statutory requirement for children by the age of eleven years (Key Stage 2) to have kept and used sketchbooks will no doubt exercise us if we have not used them before. It will cause us to wonder at what age they should be introduced, and at the most simple level, what they should be filled with.

Teachers who have made a habit of using them with their children will know of the richness and value they can embody, provided their real purpose is considered. As to the age of introduction to this work, there are examples of very interesting and enjoyable practice taking place as early as five years old. Children love to draw in their own personal books, and provided this is not seen as an alternative to all the creative art experiences in drawing and painting which should go on in early years, it can be a very valuable experience.

Books which are in common use for news, and drawing and writing, are in fact closely allied to sketchbooks provided that the teacher challenges the children to be involved in original thinking and work. Sketchbooks should be seen especially but by no means exclusively in the context of first-hand experience - and building up the habit of seizing every opportunity to look, to perceive, to draw, to make notes, can be a powerful education tool.

Sketchbooks can be purchased or made. A number of teachers have introduced unlined exercise books, while others enable children to make their own, carefully choosing different kinds of paper to be included, and the most appropriate proportion and size. (To make books entirely out of newsprint or kitchen paper would limit the quality of the work and the range of experience.) There is in fact no magic about any particular book, or in seeing that the child fills it, without thinking of the underlying purpose for which it is intended.

Artists and designers keep sketchbooks for very good reasons, filling them with collections of drawings and annotations because it helps them to think, to find out, and build up relevant source material for their work. Sketchbooks can be gold mines. We have only to open the sketchbooks of Leonardo da Vinci, Henry Moore, or J.M.W. Turner to see that they were not just so many pretty pictures, but powerful working documents.

What happens in our sketchbooks can pertain to the past, the present, and the future.

The past can be seen in relation to memory, or in working drawings and notes which at a future date can be used. Hopefully the content can offer us relevant information of an experience no longer available to us.

The present is relevant to a wide range of issues: drawing being used as a form of thinking - of exploration - of coming to terms with difficulties and problems of selection and rejection, and in finding out the ways things work.

Drawing in its broadest terms can be seen as a voyage of discovery, as we experience through the elements of art the subject matter before us - the line, colour, shape, pattern, texture and tone; selecting whichever of these we find appropriate to the task in hand. Drawing can be used as a tool for designing or for trying out ideas, experimenting, and building up alternatives in

7 years. 13.5 x 16.5 cm

Girl. 20 x 29.5 cm

ways of working - developing - assessing and evaluating what is happening, or what has happened, extending or modifying what has been done.

Drawing can be seen as a means of building up a vocabulary of ways of working, and in amassing visual information about ways of thinking and our knowledge of the environment.

Drawing can be for the sake of drawing! - for enjoyment and celebration which need not be translated into words for its validity.

For *the future*, we can take into consideration particular projects and pieces of work which are going to be undertaken. The need will be to select relevant information for this known future, and to record it, together with some thoughts and notes about how it might be used if necessary.

There are times when dictionary definitions can sharpen our understanding of the words we often use, and it seems apposite to consider a short list in the context of sketchbook practice.

Boy, 9 years. 17.5 x 16.5 cm

Exploration	The art of searching.
To explore	To search, or travel through for the purpose of discovery; to examine thoroughly.
Experiment	Experience; a trial; something done to discover something unknown, or to test a theory; to try out new styles or techniques.
Record	To set down in permanent form, to call to mind a witness; a remembrance.
Search	To scrutinise; to probe; to explore with a view to finding something; to examine closely; to put to test.
Research	Careful search; investigation; systematic investigation towards increasing the sum of knowledge; to search again.
Celebrate	To do something enjoyable because of a feeling of pleasure at some event or achievement.

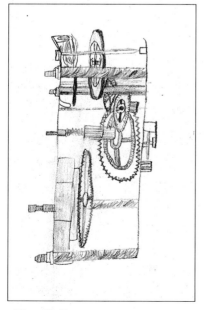

15 x 19.5 cm

Boy, 10 years. 16 x 16 cm

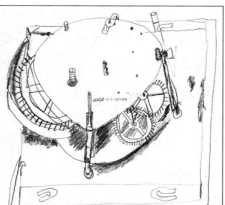

Study of a violin

POTENTIAL SUBJECT MATTER FOR SKETCHBOOKS

The short answer to this question could well be 'everything', but to offer some general stimuli the following list has been included. It is above all the first-hand experience which will be of most value, together with personal memory and imaginative involvement.

1 The elements of art

Opportunities for children to enjoy, explore, experiment, celebrate, create and record colour, line, tone, shape, pattern, texture in any or all of their diverse forms, including those within the contexts outlined below.

2 Environment

The living world, nature, the countryside, land, sea, air, the world of plants, atmosphere, weather, town and country, structures, buildings (outside or inside), machinery. Opportunities for children to work from first hand experience, memory, imagination or fantasy, the world they live in, or the stimulation of ideas from stories, poems, music. Consideration of scale - the vast and the minute.

3 People and other living things

Family, friends, self, animals, insects, birds, fish, situations, groups, individuals. Character, mood, individual and group dynamic. Personal experience.

4 The world beyond us

Life, death, dreams, legends and fantasy, the world of the unknown and inexplicable.

This may seem to offer a vast choice, and children's interests may be wide-ranging throughout their school careers. However it could be equally valid for them to concentrate on a particular aspect, and to explore and research it in depth over a period of time.

The final criteria for judgement in regard to the value of the whole experience must surely be based on the evidence of the sketchbook's content: does it show personal commitment and thinking? Is it a useful tool in the hands of the young artist or designer? Is it something he or she enjoys, and takes pride in?

For the teacher sketchbooks can proved invaluable as a means of understanding the child's thinking; and can also be a useful form of evidence in the context of assessment and evaluation.

STUDIES OF GEESE MOVING

Rachel LeGros. 7 years.

1 Previous experience

Drawing with a variety of tools and materials at home and at school. The work at home was mainly based on imagination and fantasy. This particular outing was the first time Rachel had drawn from first hand experience, and she took to it with great interest and concentration.

2 The work

On a visit to a Field Centre Rachel, who was equipped with drawing pencils, a sharpener, a piece of hardboard, a bulldog clip and a number of pieces of thin cartridge paper offcut, was much taken with a flock of white farmyard geese as they strutted, preened, fed, slept, honked menacingly or swam in the pond.

It was suggested that as they were constantly on the move a useful way to study them was to sit for some time just looking and letting them settle without trying to draw at all.

When she felt ready (which in fact was about seven minutes later), she was advised to concentrate on one goose and begin a small drawing. When that particular bird changed position a new drawing of the same, or another bird might be started... and then another... This procedure should be followed until a bird returned to a position, in which case a drawing could be continued. It was made clear to her that the important thing was the looking, and that it did not matter what the drawings looked like so long as she was finding out about the geese, their shapes and movements. It might well be that there would be no more than a whole collection of 'goose lines'. She was asked not to try to continue a bird from memory at this stage, but to concentrate on what she could see and get down before the next movement. A number of sheets of paper were covered over a period of deep concentration which lasted approximately 35 minutes. She was not interrupted at all as she worked.

3 Value

Challenge to do some high-power looking. Involvement in seeing, working from direct experience rather than memory and what she thought she saw. Using the elements of line and shape. (This in fact was the way she chose to respond, practically, and was not discussed before she began.)

4 Possible developments

Further drawing of the same kind. Developing the idea of movement in sketchbook. The same kind of challenge using other drawing tools - pens, brushes, twigs, fingers. Looking at artists' sketchbooks, or those from an upper school. Looking at Chinese brush drawings. Using the information gained to build up paintings, drawings, collages, prints, models. Taking small amounts of clay in polythene bags out to do some direct modelling on the spot. (This could as well precede the drawing activity as follow it. It is a mistake to think that interpretation into two dimensions is necessarily an aid to three dimensions - for some children it is just the opposite.)

Studies of geese moving.
Rachel LeGros, 7 years.
29.5 x 22.5 cm

28

CAT DRAWINGS

Edward and William.
Twins, 9 years.

Medium: pencil

Both boys spend a lot of time drawing, and have always been encouraged at home and school. On a visit to a relative they sat in the garden and drew the cat, who was sitting by the pond. It was interesting to see the differences in their approach. William was clearly involved in some very careful looking - with sensitive awareness of the lines which described the head, body, fish and surrounding plants. The heron trip wires have been included as part of the seen picture. He has begun to come to terms with the tonal qualities of the cat's fur. Edward moved directly into an assured 'cartoon' approach using his own imagery, and transferring the cat into his own back garden, sitting beside their own pond.

Edward 38 x 55 cm

William 26.5 x 37 cm

In conversation some months later they both remembered the drawings, and were well aware of the ways in which they had chosen on that occasion to interpret the subject matter. 'That was the sort of cartoony one I did, wasn't it?' Edward reminisced.

Many children are well aware of a variety of different ways of drawing, and can move from one mode to another at will. They are also able to make judgements using different criteria when they are intro-duced to the fact that different purposes underlie different kinds of work. In the case of these drawings, one is a sensitive and searching investigation of the cat and her surroundings, and the other is a search for symbols and character-istics to present her in caricature form. The operative question to the children is 'What have you in fact done?' The work should not be compared, but 'read', and considered for what it is.

29

HOUSES, BUSES AND A HORSE

Mark. 12 years.
Downes Syndrome.

Special School.

1 Previous experience

2 The sequence of work

A large proportion of children go through a symbolic and schematic stage of development or phase of working. Children with special educational needs are no exception, although it is possible that some of them may reach the stage later and remain in it for longer. It is by no means exceptional for some children to continue to work fruitfully in this mode continually, enjoying the build up of meticulous detail or developing strong elements of colour, pattern and decoration. Symbolism and the use of personally evolved schema are valid ways of making art forms and one only has to look at Egyptian wall paintings, or the work of Paul Klee or Marc Chagall, to realise that they can embody great aesthetic quality, beauty, skill and interest.

Opportunities for the exploration of materials, drawing, painting, collage, and modelling activities.

Mark, a lively interested child, loved drawing with linear tools and day by day drew the things which were of current interest to him in his notebook. He told his teacher of his particular interest, and she wrote them down for him on the page opposite the drawing. He then made a copy of what had been written, word for word under each line. This particular sequence covered the period of approximately one month, at a time when Mark was deeply involved in an interest in buildings with 'lots of windows', and he drew them at every opportunity. The buildings - houses, high rise flats, and office blocks - were talked about; people lived there, his father worked there, he would like to live there, he would like to work there.

The drawings, a selection of which are shown here, emerged day by day, being undertaken with interest and a methodical and businesslike working method. There were at least thirty multi-windowed drawings in this particular book before any change in schema became apparent.

Figs 1 - 3 are examples from this phase. All of the early drawings were based on upright rectangles and lovingly and rhythmically filled with windows, each of which had a cross, dividing the window into four panes. Mark worked from the top left hand corner and filled in the windows in lines across the building, in the same way in which one would build up a written page, proceeding from left to right to the bottom of the rectangle.

Figs 4 - 5 show the beginning of the change. Just under half way down the building, he stopped drawing the windows, then thoughtfully drew a central door, and two small windows flanked by two large ones at ground floor level. The drawing was considered finished.

Fig. 6. The building drawn on the following day showed less meticulous care than was typical of Mark's normal style, but the procedure was identical to that outlined previously. However, on this occasion two humanoid forms are placed 'in' the building.

Fig. 7. This is a repeat, possibly a consolidation of what had gone on the day before. There is the addition of a roof shape, a chimney and smoke. (These items have appeared in earlier drawings too.)

Fig. 8. The rectangle is drawn as usual. One window is drawn, this time with a cross and a diagonal; three figures are added, together with some items (unknown) and untypically the remaining space is filled with scribble.

Fig. 9. The building schema is drawn and five figures are added.

Fig. 10. A horizontal rectangle appears for the first time. He adds a number of circles denoting wheels and headlights, making it into the school bus. These wheels are at the top and bottom of the rectangle which makes it quite probable that Mark is using it in his own mind as a symbol for both elevation and plan. Two figures are inserted to become driver and passenger - possibly himself.

Fig. 11. The bus schema has become more sophisticated: it now has a bonnet, a door (opening outside the rectangle), luggage on the outside at the back, a driver and eleven passengers.

Fig. 12. The basic bus schema has been repeated, although of a different proportion to previous drawings. The door has a cross motif which could denote that it has glass in it. A window is set in the line of the outside wall (or possibly the roof?). There are two small windows on the outside (open or opening?). The wheels are for the first time seen as from the front, showing the raised shape of the hub cap. The bus is full of children and adults, and the driver, Mark said.

Fig. 13. The rectangle schema is repeated, but to very different effect. It would be impossible for us really to know whether the new subject matter was in Mark's mind before he began to draw, or whether he began with his usual rectangle and used it for a different purpose. What is significant is that he is using his own drawing 'language' to communicate, or perhaps celebrate something he found to be of interest or importance.

This drawing, he told us, is of himself horse riding. The rectangle is the horse's body, its head is on the left, its tail on the right. There were four helpers on his first ride, who stood on either side of the horse so that he would not fall off. Their heads, hair, legs and feet are clearly drawn. In his own mind he is on the horse, and has not therefore considered it necessary to draw himself in.

3 Value

As with any drawing experience where children are encouraged to think for themselves, there is an intermixing of personal response, thinking, selecting, organising, making, modifying. This is all set in the context of experience of tools and materials, and is the very stuff of the education process. It is very important to give children the wherewithall to be able to handle the challenges of living in the present day. It is very important as we work with children with learning difficulties that we use every aspect of their ability and the means of harnessing all modes and experiences of learning.

Note. The choice of appropriate tools for children who have physical disability of any kind is a crucial matter, and there are no simple answers. Graphic tools can liberate some, as can be seen by Mark's enjoyment and control of biros and fibre tips, while those with poor sight or inability to exert much pressure can respond well to the challenge of a good range of oil pastels, with their strong colour qualities. The painting, drawing or modelling materials used must offer self-reward in handling and in visual and tactile effect, or a large part, if not all, of the value of the experience can be lost.

The sequence of 13 drawings shows Mark's schema developing from buildings to buses, and finally to a horse

1   2   3   4

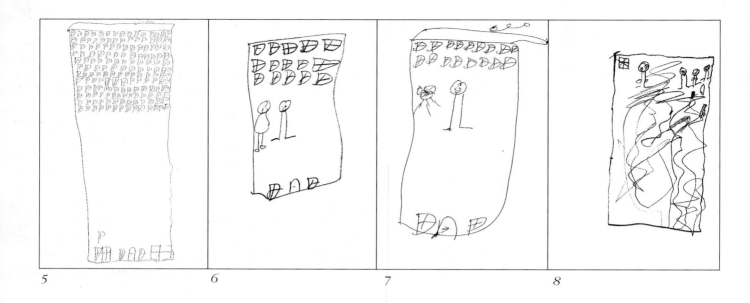

5   6   7   8

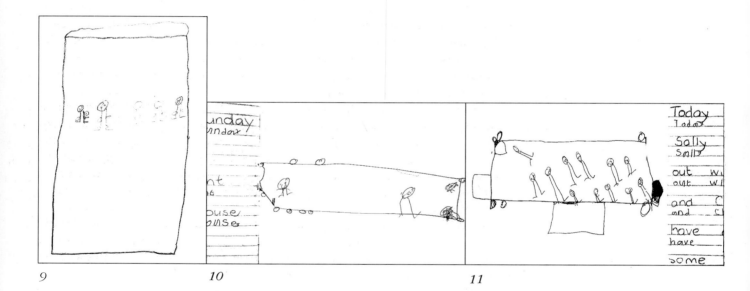

9   10   11

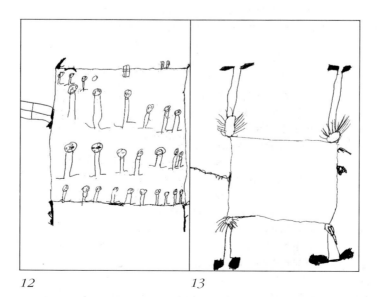

12   13

6 SELF-MOTIVATION: OUT-OF-SCHOOL ART

Many children draw, paint, model, construct, and use media and materials creatively in their own time. This area deserves our attention. It may well be that some of our pupils are far more experienced than we are aware. Some teachers have said that they had no idea of the work children were doing outside school until some circumstance brought it to their notice.

The relevant age range begins as soon as a child can make marks, and continues to the time they leave our particular class or school. Most children will have had experience of scribbling and drawing at home before playgroup or school entry, and some will also have painted, modelled, collaged and constructed. A few parents will keep children's work, some collecting almost everything the child has done. These offer us some very interesting evidence in looking at children's sequence of development and understanding, and sometimes show a very different path to the general theories of development of imagery.

The work undertaken at home may well continue alongside the school experience, and is sometimes different in nature, calibre and commitment to that which went on in the classroom. Some children can be quite articulate about the differences, and the reasons for them, including why they have not taken the work to school. Where the school is supportive an excellent degree of interaction is often apparent, and the learning which goes on in school is assimilated into personal interests and enthusiasms.

Many children can involve themselves in depth and can show considerable staying power, which may last a matter of days, weeks, months or even years, filling up sheets of paper and sketchbooks with an endless stream of activity based on their chosen interest or theme.

The following examples help gain insight into this private world.

SIMON WHITNALL
12 years. Continually drawing

A large number of small detailed drawings of lifeboats and fire engines, trains, steam engines and other kinds of machinery.

Media - biro, fibre tip, pencil and crayon. The family lived near the fire, rail and lifeboat station, and the drawings showed a strong interest in the way things were put together and worked.

The story of Simon's first day at school is told by his mother. On meeting him after school she accepted a small, scrubbed somewhat miserable watery 'lollipop' tree forlornly placed in the middle of a large piece of paper. 'That's different for you', she said. 'Yes, that's what they want there', was the reply. This was surprising, as she knew the school was very open to the children's own responses. 'Why do you say that?' she asked. 'Because', rejoined Simon, 'the girl next to me did one and the teacher said that it was very good.'

When Simon left school he took a number of different jobs, including part time fireman. He gained a place as a mature student on a BTEC General Art and Design course, followed by a BA Hons. course in silversmithing and metalwork at Camberwell College of Art. He plans to set up his own workshop. Of his present sculpture he says, 'Through drawing, photography, writing and poetry I can extract information from items found, which acts as a direct influence for my

Tractors and cars. 3 years

Fire engine. 3 years

Steam roller. 7 years

Fire engine. 8 years

Drawing made after seeing woodland fire. 8 years

Motorbike. 10 years

ADULT WORK

Detail of 'Fire vase'

'Drift and groove'. Forged steel

Detail of 'Fire vase'. Copper and forged steel

work.... Placed in relevant situations the sculptural forms aim directly to address and promote the meaning and atmosphere of the area. I believe that it is important that people can participate in the mysteries that forms/objects can generate through vision, touch, weight and sound, all of which will be affected by the natural elements and seasons.'

He says that his early childhood interests still continue.

JANE KAY
7 - 11 years
Birds of a variety of sizes and colours

Media: pencil, pen and ink, water colour, fibre tip.

The work in small sketchbooks was based on Jane's deep interest in bird life, and she spent much time making lists of birds seen. A number were copied from bird identification books, but many more were done from memory or looking at the bird table she had constructed with the help of her father. Some writing was included - in the main descriptive, or copied from the books, but including careful notation of birds seen, the date and place.

School work during her eighth and ninth year did not show any of the qualities which were so lovingly apparent in the home interests. 'Couldn't do art at school' she said. 'The paints were all messed up and dirty, and the brushes were all tatty. ... I didn't take them (the books) to school until last year, they'd have only got lost or something. In this class it's different. When I took them in Mrs W. was really interested - she asked me if she could show the others - they liked them too ... it ended up with me, Joanne, Tracy and Sarah having a sort of bird club. ... We made that bird table' (pointing out of the window). 'Would you like to look at our diary? We've collected some books too ....'

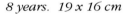
8 years. 19 x 16 cm

5 years. 14 x 13 cm

BIRD SKETCHES

6 years. 12 x 14 cm

11 years.
17 x 15 cm

9 years. 31 x 29 cm

12 years. 21 x 30 cm

THE DATE BOX CAMEL

Edward Doran, 7 years
Caroline Doran, 4 years
Rebecca Turner, 3 years

The children asked for paper and felt tips. Edward made a freely interpreted 'copy' of the picture on the cover of a box of Oasis dates, which included a camel, palm trees and buildings. The girls watched him with interest and joined in on their own version of the imagery, looking it seemed mainly at his drawing, and not often at the original stimulus.

Rebecca's camel began to take shape, and her enjoyment of the hump was repeated sixteen times in rhythmical pattern form. The legs received the same treatment and numbered twenty one. The saddle became a black-centred sun shape with red rays, and the rider appears below the camel.

Caroline appeared to be attuning to Rebecca's imagery, moving toward a freely drawn pattern approach, although the head, hump, leg and saddle/sun motifs were recognisable. In subsequent drawings she often placed the sun motif in the middle of whatever she was drawing - including human and animal forms. It is an interesting example of differing motives, with the boy attempting to depict a camel and rider reminiscent, if not a copy, of the original printed label, whilst the girls enjoyed the symbolism, patterning, and enjoyment of tools and colour. All three were pleased with their efforts.

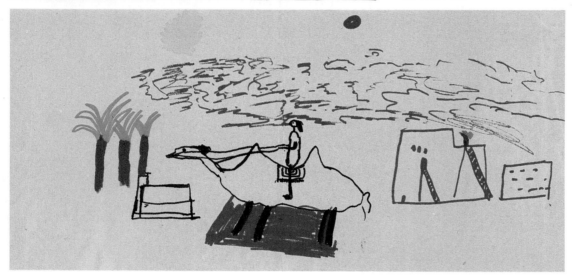

Camel and rider. Rebecca.
25 x 32 cm

Camel and rider. Edward. 31 x 62 cm

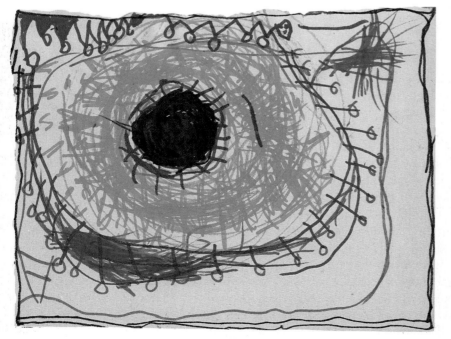

Camel and rider. Caroline. 25 x 32 cm

Margaret with the sun in her belly.
Caroline. 28 x 18 cm

26 x 35 cm

17 x 57 cm

45 x 48 cm

25 x 25 cm

Rachel Petty
5 years

Rachel has drawn and painted all her life, and she has been encouraged to do so by her parents. Her father is an art educationist, painter and printmaker, and she is used to seeing him at work, often asking for tools and materials to work alongside him. His paintings and prints are rich in colour, and often abstract in form.

She is very serious about her art, becoming totally involved, and needing little or no encouragement to proceed to what she deems to be a finished piece. She will on occasions make a request for a particular colour or tool which may not have been supplied, but which she knows to be available.

At home she seems to be totally involved in colour and shape, seldom moving toward figurative work. The paintings when she is working at the same time as her father are her own statements, and she shows no effort to copy his work, but there are apparent echoes of elements he is making use of. She works, by her own choice, in silence, but enjoys general chatter, and comments about what she is doing in pauses and coffee breaks. Conversation about the work is generally reflective in regard to the elements it is made up of. 'I like that colour' ... 'that's a nice shape.'

Immediately on finishing a piece of work she is inclined to leave it, and move away to do other things. On returning later, she looks at what she has done and usually shows great pleasure in it, enjoying talking about it and sharing it with others.

There seem to be two very definite modes of operation involved. The first is the 'making', and the second is in being able quite naturally to distance herself from it and 'appraise'. (If this seems to be too academic a word for the process in relation to this young child, or one with overtones of a more sophisticated curriculum approach, we may do well to reverse our thinking and see what a very natural procedure appraisal can actually be!) It is possible that she is at least in some part influenced by her father's practice of standing back and considering what is happening in his work, but it is quite certain that for her it is normal and useful rather than a learned, imitative meaningless response.

Rachel has been surrounded by original art and design forms in her home from birth, with a large proportion of the richly coloured prints of Michael Rothenstein, and paintings by Brian Pearce.

Bethan Barker
8 years

Bethan drew at home from the time she could manipulate a drawing tool. She was never specifically asked to draw, but tools and materials were always available. She now attends a school in an industrial city and is encouraged to work creatively. She loves reading and enjoys stories of all kinds.

Recently she has become very keen on making up her own narratives at home, and presenting them by means of drawings and written storylines. These 'books' consist of anything up to thirty pages and show the same care and involvement from beginning to end. They usually cover a number of adventures and happenings to a group of school friends, all of whom are lovingly depicted in every picture. She said that in fact only one of the figures, a Chinese girl, was based on a real person. She had been a friend who moved away to another school, and this was a way to remember her. All the others are from imagination, or reminiscent of story book characters. Her chosen medium at present is felt tip coloured pens. She has great pleasure in inviting her friends and family to read her 'books'.

Bethan's characters. 21 x 29.5 cm

That day they had to go to the docters for ingektions there mums Went with them they Set off and they waited a long time.

1 *They go for injections*

one by one they Went to docter Hills and docter cornely. (and other docters)

2 *Doctor's surgery*

Because they Were Brave the Went to the sweet shop

Tata sweet shop ....

3 *Reward!*

42

MY HOUSE AND GARDEN
Faye Turner, 6 years

This is an example of a child who enjoys drawing at home, beginning to develop an idea with an adult relative. The whole thing took off in her imagination and motivated her over a number of days.

Faye built up a word game when motoring in rural Suffolk. She had said that she wished that she lived in the country, and this led to discussion: what kind of house would she like? Would it have a garden? The idea really took hold, and she poured out lists of things she wanted to include. Most of them were seen from the car window or based on memories of the village where she was staying, together with things she had seen and experienced at other times.

'... A house with a thatched roof ... a porch with red roses on it - like that one ... a summer house to play in ... a river and a pond and some frogs... I've seen some frogs ... and fish... a pebbly path and a bridge ... a willow tree - like yours ... an orchard with apples and a swing ... a wood where rabbits live ... and a fox - we saw a baby fox when we were out walking last week ... a rose garden, and grass, and strawberries ... carrots ... lettuces ... lots of flowers - primroses and bluebells ... and a little pony.'

On returning to the house she wrote out her list, and decided she would like to draw it. She did so the next day, taking approximately three quarters of an hour. The following day she spent another quarter of an hour, finishing it to her own satisfaction. Her chosen medium was conté crayon.

What she had undertaken was, in fact, a design/drawing to her own brief.

House and garden. Faye Turner. 38 x 55 cm

Jessamy Barker
11 years

Jessamy has always been interested in physical pursuits and has involved herself fully in games and other sporting activities from an early age. She belongs to swimming and gymnastics clubs and is very much aware of the quality of movement and need for body control which is so important in these disciplines. She enjoys drawing and spends a lot of her own time depicting happenings and activities in relation to human beings.

These drawings come from a collection using subject matter based on the seasons, sports, drama and mythology (the latter including centaurs and mermaids). The last drawing in the series, entitled Gym, was undertaken after the movement sequences had been experienced at her club.

The first drawing in the lower right hand corner did not please her, and on her next visit to the library she found a book on gymnastics which seemed to her mind to be much more successful than her own. She therefore erased this particular part of the drawing and made a copy of the movement sequence from the book. Clearly there is an influence in the mode of following a figure through the various stages commonly used in gymnastics manuals, but there also seems to be a quality of understanding, the feeling of actually experiencing the movements for herself.

There is evidence from faint rubbed out figures in the top line, that she has selected and then rejected other parts of the movement sequence before coming to a final conclusion.

Gym. Jessamy Barker. 21 x 29.5 cm

David Downes.
To 11 years, and student work

David drew before he could communicate by means of words, finding a powerful means of communication when he discovered tools which enabled the precision he found rewarding - biros, fibre tips and pencils. He had found nothing but terrible frustration when challenged to use large brushes and thick paint mixtures.

His mother saved many of the drawings, and these numbered over six hundred by the time he was ten years old. A selection of the work was used in an exhibition which presented children's drawings in sequence. The evidence of the work showed in a very clear manner the relationship of David's thinking to the subject matter, and the very different insight one could gain by looking at a chronological series of pieces as opposed to the limited horizons of single drawings. (This is a practical example of the value of sequential evidence, in the form of actual pieces of work which could be seen in the context of school coursework and its assessment and monitoring.)

The exhibition, entitled 'Six Children Draw' which was sponsored by the University of London Institute of Education and Suffolk Education Authority, was supported by the publication *Six Children Draw*, edited by Sheila Paine. David was a boy of powerful enthusiasms. He was deeply interested in tall buildings and structures as a young child - windmills, pylons, highrise blocks, church and other towers. The fact that he lived in rural Suffolk and had grandparents in Walsall fed these interests. He did not draw from life, but somehow stored information in his memory, reproducing it some days later. He had a very strong feeling for visual depth (which should not be confused with mathematical perspective). He did not in fact have a photographic memory, and often a number of different aspects of the buildings he remembered was brought together in a single piece of work.

He also built up a fantasy world of named towns and cities and the events in them - Trottingham, Sizeburgh, and Clantonvane were favourites.

When he was seven years old he was given a calendar of paintings by John Constable. This proved to be very significant for him. 'I liked Constable pictures so much,' he said some years later, 'he drew so nicely with paint.' He avidly collected Constable reproductions, pressing his family to find more for him. His work, which had been almost entirely linear, broadened to include areas of colour. The paintings which were carried out in water colour were not copies of Constable, but were clearly David's beloved local landscapes influenced by what he had admired in Constable's work.

The family, unable to find more Constable paintings, gave him some other artist's work, and he moved his allegiance first to Lowry, and later to Turner, followed at a later date by David Gentleman. In each case, without any adult discussion or intervention, David's own work showed quite clearly his present interest. It seemed to be a direct non-verbal assimilation of the imagery and handling of the elements, influences of which would appear in his own drawing and painting, immediately or over the next weeks.

The atmospheric qualities which began to appear were no doubt heightened by his deep and lasting interest in the weather. When he was eight years old, weather forecasts, temperature charts, rain gauges and clouds were studied daily; and the experience of storms and the sky was to be both celebrated and dreaded.

At school David was encouraged, but whilst being co-operative he found it difficult to conform to working to specific tasks at specific times. He always tried to do so, but the quality of the work often lacked the drive and life of the independent work undertaken at home. It was not only a matter of time, as many of the drawings at home were carried out in the space of a few minutes.

At secondary school he was encouraged to draw independently in his sketchbooks as well as undertake the course requirements. David is now an art student, well into his training, and is as deeply involved in his very personal approach to art as he ever was. He has gained many more influences, and has enjoyed the course.

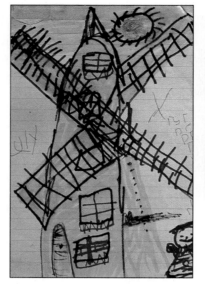

5 years

4 years

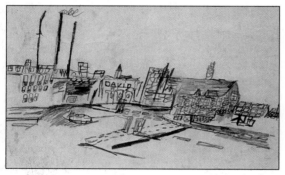

6 years

Eye church. 7 years

7 years

After seeing Constable reproductions. 7 years

After seeing Lowry reproductions   7 ³/₄ years

In the garden - direct painting. 9 years

Memory drawings, local landscape, and Walsall

9 years

9 years

Rooftops

City scene

*Illustration for an
E M Forster short story*

Portrait sketch

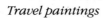

Travel paintings

The examples of his early work shown here raise a number of explicit and significant points of interest for teachers and educationists.

1 His practical exploration and experience of what tools and materials can do, which in David's case was self-motivated through interest in the subject matter. For him they were very much a means to an end, and not an end in their own right.

2 His interest in subject matter relating to his environment and surroundings. It really did move him, and he was keen to involve himself further.

3 The powerful drives of his personal interests, which enabled him at times to make leaps, developmentally.

4 Evidence of practical learning (as seen in the work) by means of steeping himself in the work of artists - Constable, Lowry, Turner and Gentleman - albeit only through the use of reproductions of a fairly small scale.

5 His ability to make practical connections between the fine art reproductions he was excited by and his own work. When David left school he was accepted on a BTEC General Art and Design course. Later he went to Cambridge Polytechnic School of Art and took a Higher National Diploma, specialising in illustration, following which he went to Brighton University for a Postgraduate course in Sequential Illustration. He is deeply interested in his work and is drawn toward the travel and reportage businesses when considering openings.

In talking of his childhood art David says, 'The interests I had then are still there. They never really go away. In fact they have become closer to me than in my teenage years when other pressures seem to take over.'

While the number of children who are as dedicated to drawing as these are in the minority, their practice can lead to some insights into the ways in which they and others, given the materials and encouragement at school and at home, could develop. There are in fact very few children who do not respond to tools and materials for their own enjoyment and interests if given the opportunity. This of course brings to the fore the importance of parents' attitudes to creative work and play. It is well worth communicating to them something of the value of all sorts of art experience, ranging from play with tools and materials, from the youngest child's scribbles, to the many trials and apparent errors which lead to development, eventual control and personal statement.

Many children involve themselves in the painstaking copying of what the teacher may well see as banal imagery, using poor cartoon modes or other mass media stimuli. It is important to respect whatever the children choose to do at home in their own time, and to help them make judgements in terms of their own criteria. If they are attempting to make copies, do they think they are good? Why, or why not? Encouragement to look at all different kinds of images and some good cartoon drawing may be a useful interest which could extend a narrow view.

Where there is a sound broad-based approach offered at school, with experience of looking at all kinds of art and ways of making it, the children should be well aware that there are many different kinds of drawing, and will not be damaged by a sortie into second-hand imagery. In fact they are communicating their interest in wanting to make images. Some television programmes successfully encourage children to make things, and of their kind can be very well communicated and sound, building up specific skills. Educationally the limitation lies in the fact that the end products have been designed by adults and require little or no thought on the part of the child, but it would be a pity if children did not feel confident enough to show or talk about what they were interested in doing or proud of having done. The criteria of judgement may well be based on the success of the skills, and a good teacher can very often draw ideas from the child, extending his or her vision of other ways to use the specific techniques and ideas undertaken. One 'put-down' of an interest is enough to stop the child ever again thinking of sharing a personal enthusiasm.

Children need only the most basic of tools and media. At the minimum, drawing tools and a good supply of paper. To extend this to allow a rounded experience, the addition of paints and brushes, mixing plates or palettes, paint, paper, malleable materials, safe adhesives and scissors, and a collection of found natural and made items are riches for creative work. There are also some interesting ranges of water soluble pencils, fibre and felt tipped pens, conte and wax crayons on the market which can enrich and add to the basic range. It is good for children to be encouraged to look after their own tools from the earliest possible age.

The joyous exploration, experimentation and celebration of colour, line, pattern, texture, shape, form and tone is evident in the work or play of children, provided they have good quality tools and materials to hand which are rewarding as opposed to being frustrating to use. This must be seen in the context of other needs - those of time and a place in which to work. The most important ingredient, however, is encouragement, in the first place on the part of the parents; and teachers (if they are aware of what is going on) can play a positive part.

It is very interesting to see the influence on children of siblings or adults in the family who practise art. It would appear that the effect ranges from the best kind of imitation, where tools and materials are used with confidence, and personal imagery developed, to a shying away from certain areas of subject matter as being far too difficult to undertake.

It is always important to encourage children to enjoy all kinds of pictures and illustrations, so that they naturally become aware of the many different ways of making art, rather than growing up with a view that it should fall within a narrow band of so called realistic, or photographic response. Consideration of the many interesting children's story book illustrations can also add to the breadth of the experience.

Although the use of sketchbooks in school may be seen as synonymous with these experiences, they are in fact very different. In the work undertaken at home the child is in full control of what to do, what to include, or exclude. Adults need to be very sensitive to the child's need for autonomy. In an ideal world the two approaches might be seen as a whole, but we must be careful to leave full responsibility for out-of-school personal work with the child.

Early drawing

Us having tea. Pencil and crayon

Pencil drawing

The bee. Watercolour

Pen and ink

School. Watercolour

Painted screen. Student work.
140 x 180 cm

Jesus in the house of Simon. Etching

Wall painting, Laverdin. Oil.
36 x 24 cm

Living in peace. Etching

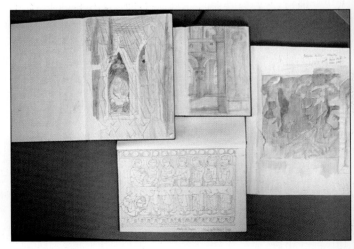

Adam and Eve, Easby. Oil. 36 x 60 cm

Atlantes, Aulnay. Etching

Sketchbooks

ARTISTS AND THEIR CHILDHOOD WORK

It is always interesting to see the childhood work of adult artists. From the teacher's point of view there is magic in being able to see what really did happen later - a gift which is not allowed us with the children we teach at present. We ask ourselves constantly how effective we are being in our own educational practice, and have to come to terms with the problem of evaluating our own performance and the child's, based on criteria which inevitably lack the evidence of the clearest form of vision - that of hindsight.

There are some collections of the childhood work of artists which have been documented, but they are relatively few and far between. These include the studies of John Everett Millais, and Henri de Toulouse Lautrec (*Six Children Draw*, edited by Sheila Paine). Sheila Paine was also responsible for an exhibition of the childhood work of the cartoonist Gerard Hoffnung, entitled 'The Young Hoffnung', which was a chronological study of his early development. On meeting Annetta Hoffnung and looking at the work, she wrote 'I was astonished to discover how many drawings had been preserved. Even now when children's drawing is enjoying a new interest it is rare to find continuous sequences from any one child, even in limited numbers. Yet it is these sequences that are needed if we really want to know how children's expressive and imaginative skills develop.'

There is also a very interesting publication illustrating the work of the young Michael Rothenstein (*Drawings and Paintings. Aged 4 - 7. 1912-1917*). When looking at the work of the artist when young, it is fascinating to be able to identify interests, characteristics, idiosyncracies, content, colour choices and element dominances apparent at an early age and continuing into adult work.

A selection of the childhood and adult work of the painter and etcher Valerie Thornton, has been included as an interesting example.

Valerie Thornton
1931 - 1991

Valerie drew all her life. From the evidence of early scribbles, drawings and paintings she showed a deep interest and involvement in what was going on around her, and in the life of her friends and family. The humour and enjoyment evident in the 'Life of the Bee' with its composition based on shapes which enclose pictorial matter and decoration, is one which appears again and again in the later work. She seems to have been fascinated by the relationship of a number of figures or happenings which could be brought together within the structure of a number of confined cell-like areas.

Her interest in early Romanesque architecture, relief carving and wall paintings, which were stimuli for so many of her drawings, paintings and etchings, is developed into very personal statements by the selection of groups or units which were brought together into a single harmonious whole.

The drawing of the 'Tea Party' where her friends and family are all neatly labelled, and the food has been laid out meticulously on the long table, bears a striking resemblance to one of her last etchings. The mode of arranging compositions in a beautifully simple two-dimensional way was as effective in her adult work as it was in childhood, where, no doubt it would have been a direct symbolist response rather than a conscious choice.

Valerie worked mainly from first-hand stimuli translated into her own reality. She was well aware that there must be a metamorphosis from the seen and assimilated experience to a very personal response and statement which is unique to the individual.

We would be mistaken if we believed that in art education our aim was only to enable children to make competent likenesses, without opening the experience of each of them to the possibilities of their own personal language of communication, expression and learning. If interests and motivation can be triggered, it is possible that they could prove to be a lifelong involvement, even if not at a professional level.

Part 2 Class and group exemplars

In the majority of the group or class exemplars presented, each 'package' of children's work has been laid out in four stages:

1 Referring to the kind of experiences the child has had prior to the particular work
2 Presenting the work
3 Offering brief insights into the value of the experience
4 Laying out possible developments which could grow from the project.

Each exemplar is reported by the class teacher or art co-ordinator.

FAMILY FIGURES

Jenny. 4 years. Nursery school

1 Previous experience

This series of paintings was not Jenny's first experience of paint. She had handled drawing tools and materials at home and play school and enjoyed vigorous scribbling. She never needed any suggestions as to what she might do, plunging into materials exploration of her own chosen subject matter the moment she picked up a drawing tool.

2 The work

Fig. 1. A direct painting on sugar paper. Carried out in a few minutes and proudly named 'A man and his dog'.

Fig. 2. This painting seems to be based on, or have evolved into a painting of her family. She is clearly enjoying exploring the idea of figures and using paint.

Fig. 3. 'This,' she said, pointing to the figures and components in turn, 'is mummy, this is daddy, this is my sister, and me, and this is the sun and a day sky, and this is the moon and a night sky.' It is interesting but not unusual to see that the figures are fitted into the spaces and are sometimes to be seen sideways or upside down. The previous painting was still in sight, which may have been an influencing factor.

Fig. 4. The content of the third painting is based on the use of the schema and symbolism of the preceding works. The fact that she was accidentally making green by not washing her brush sufficiently was not lost on her. Her comment at the end of painting, as she pointed to the top left hand corner was, 'Those are stars.'

3 Value

The particular interest in these pieces of work lie in the fact that they were carried out over a short time span in sequence, and that there is evidence of considerable experience and learning going on. 'A man and his dog' shows the organisation of two figures on the picture plain with no overlapping shapes. This is quite typical of a young child's approach.

The second painting is more complex, with Jenny building up a number of components and filling more of the space. At some point along the line, or possibly before she began, she has linked the symbols with members of her own family.

The third painting is a repeat of the basic schema she has already established, with a very strong feel for the nature of the shapes and the way they fit together. There is still no overlapping of shapes as the concept remains strongly symbolic rather than visually and analytically perceived. There is also the addition of the

2 *62 x 48 cm*

1 *A man and his dog. 62 x 48 cm*

3 *62 x 48 cm*

4 *36 x 24 cm*

My dad helps me swim

I like lemon barley

*I had a new pair of plimsolls
in the holiday*

My brother Adam is in bed - he makes a lot of noise

Mummy has just had baby Dominic

It's me in colour land

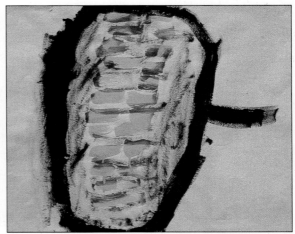

I don't like the smell of beans cooking

components of the 'sun and day sky', and 'moon and night sky'. These may well have begun as accidental marks which triggered her thinking in terms of a particular shape or 'message', but were clearly quite consciously developed and used as part of the whole once she had had the idea.

The final painting in the series repeats the schema once more - possibly consolidating her symbols, or the idea. The accidental colour mixing brings in a new piece of experience which will no doubt be put to good use in the future.

There can of course be a danger in reading deep significance into the content of children's work. There are no doubt some aspects of art therapy or psychologically based studies which can give clinical insights, but these are for the experts. For the teacher the important things to look for are the developmental patterns (or lack of them) and clues which can show us strengths and weaknesses. The evidence lies in watching the ways in which children work.

PAINTINGS AND DRAWINGS

Kelly. 6 years.
Primary school

The paintings and drawings are a selection of Kelly's work from a sequence undertaken during an autumn term. An area was set aside for up to five children to undertake creative work at any time. Tables were set up, and basic media and tools were provided - papers, collage materials, powder, tempera colours, tools.

In this school the day began with the children drawn together for a news and discussion period. This was a teacher-led discussion of whatever was relevant – perhaps things that had happened, or that we were looking forward to. This was followed by an outpouring of what they wanted to tell me. I found it very important for them to have this opportunity to get emotive issues out of their systems at the beginning of the day.

The children knew that they could use their own ideas in writing or art activities, and the order in which they undertook them could be flexible. I have always felt it important to talk to the children about the plan for the whole day and what they would be expected to do. There is a much stronger sense of purpose when the plan is negotiated to begin with. Each child knew that they would have three or four tasks. It was of course my responsibility to cover the full range of the curriculum and I could operate checks and balances where these were necessary. The 'news' stimulus was an excellent ground for art, where the strong motivational drives of personal involvement carried the techniques with them. I know that some people say that 'news' can be dull, but it depends on whether it really gets to the children's interests and realities. They would often be highly motivated to communicate ideas following the session.

Kelly's work speaks for itself. She draws and paints what she thinks, feels and wishes to express. There are a number of children whose language and involvement in other curriculum areas are brought to life by the initial experience in creative work. I found it important to talk to the children when they were painting and drawing. I often became more aware of their educational needs and ways of thinking. I could offer encouragement and stimulation and extend their experience in what they were doing in art and design. Questions such as 'Have you thought of using ...?', 'Have you tried this brush to see which is better ...?' 'Have you tried mixing ...?' If you never intervene, they can go on repeating the same things in the same way, and never move forward.

When work was finished we discussed it in order to learn everything we could from it. Much of it was displayed in the classroom, and generally talked about and enjoyed. It was often used as a basis for an assembly, where it could be shared with other classes and staff. We believed that it was important for the children to see that their work was valued.

In this school we kept a folder for each child, and a selection of work was added each half term. This included language and written work, maths, humanities and art. It was invaluable in our being able to see evidence of a sense of progression, and was very useful as a basis for discussion at parents' evenings.

PORTRAITS
1 Previous experience

First School. A class of 34 children (6 and 7 year olds).

Children are encouraged to develop learning and thinking skills through the frequent use of imagery. Drawing and painting from direct observation is a regular activity in addition to working from memory and imagination. The school acts as one of the centres for the LEA loan scheme of original works of art and design, so the children have access to a wide range of such work for source material for looking, talking and as a stimulus for some of their own work. Through this means the children are aware of the qualities of original works, such as the materials used by artists, different styles and purposes of image making, as well as historical, environmental and social implications. Their own work reflects this breadth in that they use a range of images, materials and processes in two and three dimensions with confidence and pleasure.

2 The work

Norwich Castle Museum has a commitment to educational visits. It mounts special exhibitions for schools each year, as well as providing meetings and support materials for teachers. A recent venture was a public exhibition entitled 'Norfolk Portraits' which consisted of works from local and national collections, 15th Century to today, with a complementary exhibition for young people called 'Faces'. A visit was arranged through the Museum Education Service.

Before the visit the class had spent some time observing and discussing faces, facial expressions, making comparisons of self with friends. The children brought in photographs of members of their families. Displays of children's work, alongside the photographs, built up over a period of three weeks.

I attended a teachers' meeting at the Castle Museum, to find out about the exhibitions, but felt that I needed more time there to plan the details of the visit. This meant a Sunday afternoon familiarising myself with the layout of the galleries and deciding, from the wide range of portraiture, which aspects should provide the focus. Information and worksheets, available at the museum, were helpful in giving the background, though in practice I prefer to depend as much as possible on the children's own ability to look and 'make notes' through drawings and writing.

One October morning, the children, armed with pencils, crayons and paper, were taken to the museum. The museum's Education Officer, Lynn, took half the group to see the portraits while I took the rest to see the Faces Exhibition, changing groups at half time. Some of the exhibits were self-portraits, others were from an historical period, others explored facial expressions. There were information and questions under each painting, for example:

> 'These artists have painted themselves surrounded by things that are important to them. James Sillett loved painting flowers. So did John Bratby, but he has also included his family. Laura likes being in the garden with her teddy. What would you want to have in a picture with you?'

> 'These four portraits all have plain backgrounds and similar expressions on their faces. But their clothes are very different. How is the way we look affected by what we are wearing? Would you want to wear your best clothes to have your portrait painted?'

After giving them time to browse, the group was called together to concentrate on these questions. They were asked to draw themselves and answer either of the above questions by what they included in their drawings. They put in their pictures whatever objects or clothes they felt important to them.

The children approached this with confidence, sitting or lying on the gallery floor. They drew about what they would wear and what they were going to put in their pictures. They had about twenty minutes for drawing, collecting information rather than completing pictures. Meanwhile the other half of the class observed the grouping and composition of individual and group portraits in the portrait exhibition with Lynn, who discussed the people portrayed, and invited

Elizabeth I

Drawings by children at the gallery

Luckvinda

Jay

Painting of themselves done in school after the visit

Sir Robert and Lady Buxton and child

Families painted in school after the visit

questions from the children, bringing out their understanding of why and how a painting had been set out in a particular way or how the painter had made one person look more important. This questioning made the children look more closely and become more aware of the subtleties and conventions of portraiture. They were given the opportunity to draw their favourite portrait.

The next day we were able to begin work on the development and extension of the working drawings done at the museum. The children were given a choice of media to construct large portraits of their choice e.g. paint, craypas, crayons, pencils, felt pen. The children discussed among themselves the layout and content of their picture as they worked. It was interesting to see that the portraits of themselves bore little resemblance to the small drawings. Most of them decided to change the objects for inclusion or clothing. Changes of mind in this context are a healthy sign of pupils learning to think for themselves.

Some decided to do portraits of their own families (including pets in one case) using compositional ideas seen at the gallery. Luckvinder, a girl from India, began a portrait of herself but got much more interested in the use of the paint than the image, resulting in a magnificent use of colour and texture (page 58). Jay depicted himself in a very smart suit, like a painting he saw of a solemn looking boy in a black jacket and a large white collar.

The variation in images reflected the stages of development the children had reached. Although they are of similar age, the children's portrayal of the human figure is a mixture of observation, information and experience but with a heavy dependence on their individual figure symbol.

Although work had been done before the visit about expressions and feelings, together with observations which had been made of these in the Faces Exhibition, it was noticeable that the portraits they did back at school had little regard for facial expression.

These pictures progressed over a period of days, integrated with other areas of the curriculum and particularly written work. Paper frames were made by the children for each painting and the work was displayed as in a gallery. The results looked spectacular and attracted much comment from other children and adults. Some of the children brought in their parents to look and talk about the results.

3 Value

Using actual works of art as a learning source gave children a number of experiences: the opportunity to become more acutely aware of the work of artists, a way of developing critical thinking, and the realisation of the historical and cultural context of pictures. Through discussion and their own practical interpretations children began to understand how artists think and work.

The drawings produced at the gallery included details of clothing, objects and setting beyond what I would expect from these children. On returning to school these items tended to be less important to them as their own ideas took over. On the surface it appears to be a reversion, but, from previous experience, I would expect the visit to produce enriched work in the longer term. What was very evident was the interest and strong focusing on the theme as a result of this opportunity to see real pictures.

4 Further development

Selected aspects of the experience of visiting a gallery and seeing original works of art were explored in this project. Many others would be possible: a study of a particular historical period, bringing in costume and surroundings, making comparisons with past and present, or a study of the lives of the people depicted. More detailed work could also have been done about the composition, the use of colour and the contents of the paintings, e.g. background, objects or furnishings. What was very clear was the richness of the experience and the depth of interest shown by the pupils; it opened up many potential areas for enjoyable learning by making use of 'real things' in the future.

HEADS

1 Previous experience

The projects on heads and character was part of a main project on theatre which lasted for a term. The children explored amongst other things the history of theatre and various aspects of it. They designed and made their own puppets and puppet theatre, and performed their own plays. Beforehand the children had painted self-portraits. They also made observational drawings of a friend and then identified specific characteristics which would enable them to develop the drawing into a caricature.

2 The work

In the project on theatre the children looked at character. This involved them in a variety of art activities and the use of different media.

1   The children were told in advance that they were going to work with magazine illustrations of heads. They were given the opportunity to search out and collect some for themselves, which allowed them an element of choice and made it their project. It was suggested that magazines illustrating hair styles would be a good source of heads of a suitable size. The head illustrations were cut in half. The children were to use these head halves in two ways: first for an observational and colour mixing activity in which they completed the glued-down half of the head as accurately as they could, and second for an activity in which they tried to imagine the character of the person depicted by the head half which they had chosen and tried to complete the head using colours and forms which would convey this to the viewer. Some discussion took place as to how this might be achieved, particularly noting that non-naturalistic colours and forms might be more powerful than representational ones.

2   Still within the context of character we explored the idea of imaginary 'rooms' in our head. The children were then invited to depict these in an almost life-size head outline. Some of the children were able to draw their own outline, but for those who experienced difficulty in making the outline large enough, a template was provided. A choice of either paint or aquarelle crayons was offered.

3   We also looked at the character of clowns, and particularly at the way in which clowns sometimes have to disguise their true feelings. The children designed clown heads, and then transferred the drawings to lino blocks which they cut and from which they then printed. The prints were made on to paper initially and different colourways investigated. All of the blocks were then used to print on to fabric from which to make curtains for the puppet theatre.

4   In the fourth activity the children looked at feelings and mood. As children of this age are sometimes reluctant to talk, paint or write about their own feelings it was necessary to approach this activity from a universal starting point. Maurice Sendak's *Where the Wild Things Are* was chosen. This story offered an opportunity for musical improvisation, dance, and three-dimensional work in the creation of large 'heads' to depict the character of the 'Wild Things'.

3 Value

This is egocentric activity. This makes it highly motivating, for children are always interested in their own and each other's faces. As a project it has many facets and strong links with traditions of portraiture. There is potential for work with critical studies and history.

4 Further developments

As this was a many-layered project there are some aspects of extension and development within the activities already described. However the work using half heads to 'match' in a non-naturalistic way was developed further in a critical studies context to introduce the children to the paintings of artists such as Vlaminck, Derain and Picasso.

HEADS

Portraits

10 years. 27 x 23 cm

9 year old's drawing of a
7 year old. 25 x 20 cm

7 year old's drawing of a
9 year old. 25 x 20 cm

Drawing developing to caricature

10 years. 30 x 24 cm

10 years. 30 x 24 cm

10 years. 30 x 24 cm

The 'other side' of the character

Each 23 x 20 cm

23 x 20 cm

'What goes on inside a head'

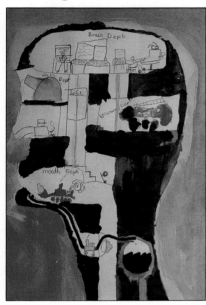

29 x 22 cm

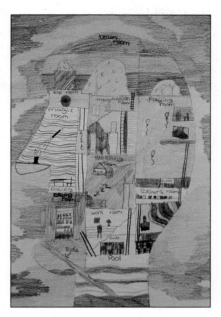

29 x 22 cm

'Clown' lino block and print

29 x 22 cm

29 x 22 cm

Masks and costumes for the 'Wild Things'

29 x 22 cm

29 x 22 cm

29 x 22 cm

1 and 1a Kristi, $8\frac{1}{2}$, and Nicky, 9, were asked to think about themselves and their particular characters, and to make a drawing from memory.

2 and 2a Two weeks later they were given mirrors and asked to look at themselves carefully, and to draw what they saw.

3 and 3a One week later they were again given the mirrors, and following some experimental work with pencils were challenged to draw a self portrait, but this time to begin with a shape (other than a feature) from within the face. All the shapes they could see, whether features or 'in-between shapes' were to be considered of equal importance. Both children began with the shape between the nose and central upper lip.

Reported by Kevin Mathieson of
Enfield Teachers' Centre, based
on inservice work in three
schools

materials. The work here shows how children have used computers, often for the first time, to explore line, colour, shape, space, pattern and texture.

Art or graphics software is available for most modern desktop computers. Essentially they consist of a drawing area, a number of drawing and painting tools, and a colour palette, with additional facilities for cutting, pasting, repeating, etc. Items are chosen by moving a mouse that controls a floating pointer on the screen. By pointing at a particular tool and clicking the mouse the tool is selected. Once an image or drawing has been produced it can be saved to disc. Indeed it is possible to save a sequence of ideas, thus documenting the history of an idea. In this sense the computer could be described as an electronic sketchbook and a tool for making changes. Images can then be printed out or recalled at a later stage and developed in different ways.

It is by understanding the strengths and limitations of using a computer that we can begin to incorporate the work into a broad and balanced art programme. It should never be seen as a substitute for working with traditional materials but as a way of extending art experience by freeing the individual from traditional constraints so that ideas can be explored freely, leading to a deeper understanding of the elements of art.

Many children want to produce realistic images on the computer, but sadly, these often look like the results of mechanical drawing aids or painting by numbers. Experimentation enables them to see potential and to control the equipment to their own ends.

Exploration
4 - 5 year olds

When we are given any new tool, be it an art tool, musical instrument or new ball, we find out what it can do. The same applies to using any art program on a computer. With this knowledge and understanding we can begin to find appropriate contexts for its use. When I have worked with children for the first time, the delight on their faces as the mouse is pressed and a line of colour

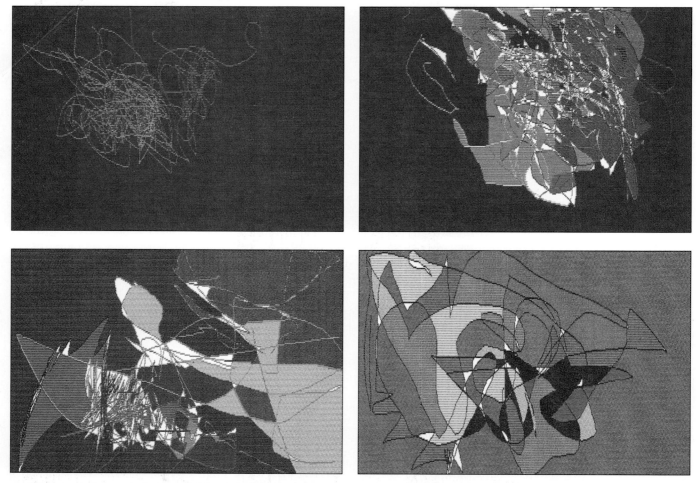

1-4 Experiments with line and fill. Reception age children

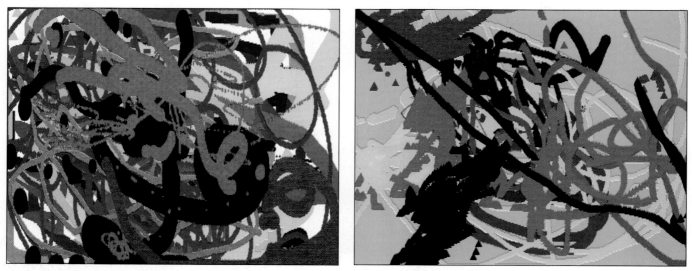

5-6 Exploring brush shapes. Reception age

7-8 Explorations. Boy, 8 years

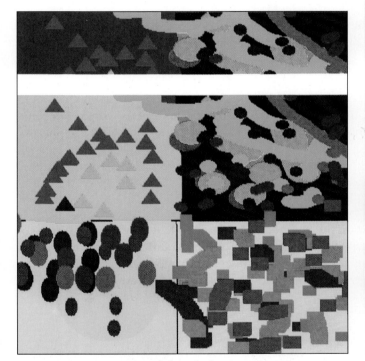

9-10 Experimenting with brush shapes. Reception age

appears on the screen is evident and they soon learn to control the process that they are involved in.

Initially I talked to the children about home computers. They described the most popular computer games and this led us into talking about creating our own pictures on the computer screen.

I started by giving a brief explanation of the computer system and then demonstrated how to use the mouse to select tools and colours from the screen.

The children worked in pairs and were encouraged to explore the tools without restraint. After this period of exploration mini challenges were set.

Challenge 1   Figs. 1, 2, 3, 4 (p.66)

'Choose the pencil tool from the menu on the screen and draw all over the screen to create interesting shapes.'

Once the tool has been selected continuous pressing of the mouse allows lines to be drawn until the button is released. Initially the children concentrated on line and on holding the mouse correctly. This progressed to the use of the fill tool, requiring the children to use the mouse to select different colours to fill the various parts of their designs. This activity took about half an hour, and in that time the children produced their own pattern picture using line, shape, space and colour. They also gained a degree of confidence in controlling the mouse and selecting items from the screen.

Challenge 2   Figs. 5, 6

'Create patterns using different brush shapes, sizes and colours'.

These images are more dynamic because of the variety of brush shapes and sizes used. The children noticed that if the mouse was moved too quickly the result would be a staggered line. This is due to the computer screen's inability to cope with rapid movement. They also discovered the excitement of wiping out one colour with another. This process in itself creates layers and can give the illusion of depth.

Figs. 7, 8 show the first explorations by an 8 year old child. Compared to the earlier images they show great confidence and an eagerness to explore the various tools available.

Experimentation
4 - 5 year olds

As the children worked on the computer we observed that they quickly began to experiment by moving into different parts of the program. This experimentation is essential to the learning process, but it does need to be given a focus so that experience leads to progression, and new skills will need to be learnt as appropriate.

Challenge 3

Experiment with different brush shapes

The children soon discovered that one click on the mouse gave the brush shape, and continuous pressing provided either a rounded or hard edged mark, depending on the shape selected.

Fig. 9. In this image it is interesting to note progression from the tentative, almost isolated triangular shapes to the use of different size brushes with some overlapping. The fill tool was used to give the different coloured backgrounds.

Fig. 10. Given the same challenge this work is more adventurous and shows not only evidence of and confidence in overlapping the shapes but also the use of the spray and watercolour facilities. A similar project with older children might focus on colour and shape through the seasons, or the elements air, earth, fire and water. At this stage only the basic tools have been used. When appropriate and when needs arise the more advanced tools like cut and paste, rotate and mirror will need further explanation and experiment. All of the children were given assistance in saving their work to disc and in printing out their final pictures. As the children gain confidence they can begin to take more responsibility for these processes.

Water project
7 - 8 year olds

This project was carried out by a group of 7 - 8 year olds with only a limited amount of experience in using the computer. I worked with the class teacher in developing their topic on water. We decided to look at how we could use the computer in three different ways - as a starting point, as part of a process and as an end product in itself. (See p. 70)

Studying paintings
7 - 8 year olds

Another challenge that children have found exciting is to choose a reproduction of a painting and initially to try and 'translate' the image using the appropriate tools. This challenge requires more ingenuity by children as they are encouraged to use their previous skills and knowledge. Obviously it is impossible to recreate the textural effects of Van Gogh's 'Sunflowers' on a computer. Texture 'in' a computer image becomes pattern, unlike the thick brush strokes created by paint. Nevertheless, it can provide an ideal opportunity to discuss the technique of the artist, leading on to a discussion of what the artist is trying to communicate. The strength and excitement of the colour yellow can be achieved as there are many shades to select from. Similarly there are numerous brush shapes that can be utilised. The image produced cannot be a replica of the artist's work but this can highlight the possibilities and limitations of using the computer for art. (See p.71)

In all cases when we looked at the work of artists we talked a lot about colour and mood. The children imagined the number of times the artist changed colours and shapes and were pleased that in using the computer they could save many versions of the same picture or even enlarge a part of it to create something totally different.

The teachers I have worked with had no previous experience of using the computer for art but worked alongside the children and as their confidence of using the basic tools increased they were more willing to explore other more advanced facilities if the need arose.

Work on the computer can add an extra dimension to making images and increases children's knowledge and understanding of how artists work. If Leonardo da Vinci had had access to a computer we would probably be paying homage to his computer pictures at galleries throughout the world!

The works were produced on a standard Archimedes A3000 Computer using Flare and Pro-Artisan software and printed out using an Integrex Colourjet 132 colour printer.

COMPUTER ART: THE WATER PROJECT

As a starting point (Fig. 11)

After initial experimentation on the computer we had a discussion with the children about the colours and shapes of movements to be found in water: turquoise blue and green, reflections of clouds, flowing, seaweed, raindrops ... The children then worked in pairs at the computer and were challenged to use the brush shapes and colours from the palette. The resulting image of seaweed is free, exciting and complex in both colour and composition.

11 Seaweed. Girl, 7 years

12a

12 Shape and colour in water. Boy, 7 years

As part of a process (Figs. 12, 12a)

Using the same starting point - shape and colour in water - this exciting computer image was then used as a starting point for a piece of weaving. A large printout of the computer image was obtained. The challenge was to identify an area of the printout and interpret it using a wide range of coloured wools and fabrics. A number of wire hoops were wrapped with wool and woven into a larger hoop to represent the droplets of water in the original image. Other looser clumps of wool were added to give the feeling of movement expressed by the patterns created by the spray facility on the computer.

13 Water. Boy, 7 years

As an end product (Fig. 13)

This image is more sophisticated and shows evidence of exploration and experiment from other challenges. A variety of tools have been used including different brush strokes and widths, continuous and staggered movements and the use of the spray facility, giving a complex layered effect. It also shows some understanding of colour in the way the different shades have been used, and is an interpretation of the colours and movement in water. As a further development the image could be used as a starting point to develop work on colour, line and shape. Children have also found it interesting to discuss each other's work to identify which aspect of the program has been used.

14 & 15 'Impressions' Boy and girl, 5-6 years

 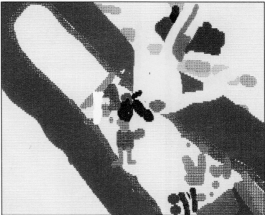

16 'The pool of London'
Boy and girl, 7-8 years

17 Enlarged section

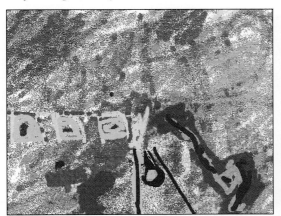 

18 Rain, steam and speed'
Boy and girl, 7-8 years

19 Enlarged section

Figs 14, 15: The children worked in pairs sketching in an outline which they then coloured using the fill tool. The images were sprayed with different shades to create an impressionistic effect. These activities gave many opportunities for language work relating to pictorial composition e.g. foreground, middle-ground, background, horizon and juxtaposition of colour.

Figs 16, 17: The interpretation of the André Derain picture 'The Pool of London' challenged the children to think about proportion i.e. the relationship between the shapes and spaces. Initially they chose thick brushes to

create instant impact but later realised that thinner ones were more appropriate.

Figs 18, 19: The children responded eagerly to a book on Turner and were keen to work on the picture 'Rain Steam and Speed'. It wasn't long before they realised how difficult this was. The resulting image shows how the children tried to portray visual depth by using different tools for the foreground and background. Clearly they captured the atmosphere of the picture and learnt a lot about how the painter worked.

1

2

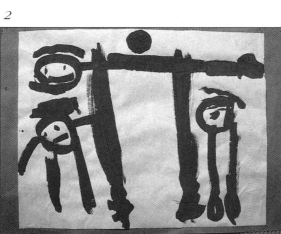

3

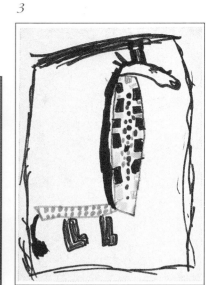

4

5

6

7

1 Studies of surfaces.
   Powder paint. 11 years

2 Horse riding. Powder paint.
   Special school. 11 years

3 Giraffe. Felt tips. 6 years

4 Museum study: pot.
   Powder paint. Girl, 8 years

5 The arrival of Rosie the Rhino
   (stuffed) at Ipswich Museum.
   Chalk and charcoal.

6 Drawing of cat, from life. Chalk
   and charcoal. Girl, 9 years

7 Brush drawing on newspaper.
   Powder colour

THE IMPACT OF THE SECOND WORLD WAR

A cross-curricular project for
9 - 11 years

Art and design: being a war artist

The Second World War project was designed by Newham Drama Team as a vehicle to help pupils and teachers across parts of the History, English, Art, Geography and Technology curriculum. Using aspects of the Second World War as a starting point, a piece of Theatre in Education was developed. The context of the programme was 'evacuation', and was particularly pertinent to the area of local studies in the East End. The programme explored the lives of three East End children and their families and took place in different locations - on a London railway platform, in a billeting hall in the country and in the village where the children were evacuated.

Problems arising out of the first half of the play allowed the pupils to become directly involved in practical tasks to help some of the characters as they struggled through the war years. During the play and in the workshops children were encouraged to develop their understanding of the Second World War experientially. This included being in 'role' as an evacuee, drawing and observing other children as homeless bomb victims, and making puppets from contemporary recycled materials.

The programme also drew comparisons with wars today, explaining how everyone suffers in war, and how it has a particular impact in making people homeless. The children were divided into several workshop groups and given $2^1/_4$ hours to complete their tasks. The resulting work was used in the second half of the play.

The workshops were of a cross-curricular nature. Those relating to Art were as follows.

Aims (linked to the National Curriculum for Art)
- to develop children's understanding that the work of artists is influenced by where and how they live and work
- to enable children to use a sketchbook to record observations
- to develop their understanding of the relationship between techniques, imagination and observation
- to experiment with the different qualities of line and tone in making and developing images.

Recording the bomb damage
At the beginning of the workshop all children were given a spiral bound sketchbook to collect information about the things they might have seen, working from resource stimuli in dramatic situations. This included a sketchbook by the sculptor Henry Moore, with reproductions of his wartime 'shelter drawings', showing Londoners sheltering from the Blitz (No. 7 overleaf), together with the famous picture of the City burning round St Paul's Cathedral (No. 1), and a photograph we obtained of an artist drawing in front of St Paul's (No. 2).

The workshop was divided into three parts. In the first the children drew the play's backdrop, a large painting based on photographs depicting the devastation and destruction caused by an air raid over London. They were asked to imagine that they were emerging from a shelter after such a raid. In this part of the session the aim was to extend their visual vocabulary and develop different methods of gathering information, enabling them to apply it at a later stage in the workshop. Two of the methods used were:

Negative drawing - covering one page of the sketchbook in charcoal lightly rubbed in, and then drawing with a soft eraser into the grey charcoal. This developed the composition through negative shapes. Depth and detail were added by using charcoal as a drawing tool.

Drawing the whole scene - the aim was to enable children to develop a whole picture of the effect of the raids in their sketchbooks by asking them to draw

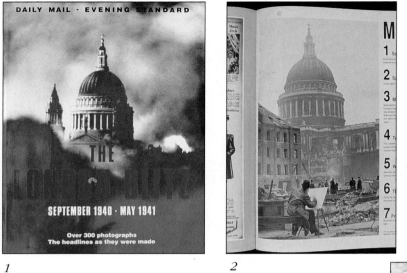

1

2

Figs. 3 - 6   Chalk and charcoal   Blitz drawings

3

4

5

6

7 Henry Moore: A shelter sketchbook

8

9

10

11

12

across the full page and then focus on a small detailed area such as an individual emerging from the rubble.

The children were encouraged to experiment with other drawing methods - smudging, drawing with dirty fingers, crumbling charcoal and black pastel on to the page, and combinations of these techniques.

The shelter pictures

The second part of the workshop involved making 'frozen pictures' or tableaux of groups of people in the air raid shelters and underground stations. Stimulus had come from the drama and an exhibition of photographs. The children were asked to think about the feelings people might have had while sheltering from the bombs. This was reinforced with lines from the play when characters complained that 'there was nowhere to go to the toilet' and that they 'couldn't get a good night's sleep', that there were 'too many screaming kids'. Some of the characters also 'enjoyed chatting' and 'having a good singsong'.

The children were divided into two groups, one acting out the scene while the others drew the situation as they imagined it in their sketchbooks. They then changed round to allow all children to do both. The drawing methods used included the linear techniques used by Henry Moore to describe shape and form.

The exhibition of Blitz pictures

In the final part of the workshop the children made 'The Exhibition' paintings. The Exhibition was to address the problem in the play where the character ARP Jenkins had to encourage more people to volunteer as air raid wardens. The object of the work was to produce a piece of 'real art' that explained what people saw and felt about the Blitz in London.

This work was not just to be advertising posters for more volunteers for the war effort; the children's work was to be evaluated as 'war artists'. They were asked to produce a monochrome drawing that explored the emotion of being caught up in an air raid. They were able to apply the knowledge they had gained from their experiments with monochrome media, and use the characteristics of the materials to develop their final work. Throughout the session there was time to discuss and evaluate, share their experiences and modify and develop their work. Finally they mounted and packed their drawings and sent them to Air Raid Warden Jenkins to exhibit in the final part of the programme.

Art and design development and progression

Teachers continued the work back in the classroom by looking at and comparing other war artists like John Sargent (the First World War artist) and John Keene (the Gulf War artist); by examining the techniques and media of war artists; by investigating parallel situations today, such as homelessness and conflict, and using them as starting points for art and design work; and by developing the use of sketchbooks for gathering information, as visual notebooks, and for ideas that progress to more substantive work.

COLLAGE EXPERIENCE

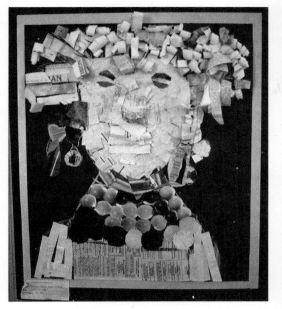

Paper collage head
'Mr Fuzz'.
Two girls, 9-10 years.
45 x 30 cm

Exploring the
qualities of paper

EXPERIENCE OF FORM: Clay

Clay is a wonderfully direct medium and work with it is based on sensory tactile experience. It can fruitfully be enriched by, but is not solely dependent on vision. In the initial stages, if visual exploration is not tempered by practical response to the qualities of the materials, it can become a stultifying factor. It is enlightening to see how children respond to clay when they are first introduced to it, provided that it is of an appropriate consistency and that they are encouraged to handle it and see what it will do. It is generally a mistake to introduce tools at an early stage, as it may well preclude experience which can teach them the full potential of the use of their own hands – the best tools of all.

If they have been led to believe that it is always necessary to make something recognisable, they may well just do that, with little thought or feeling for the medium they are using. It is often quite easy to identify these models with their tight little forms and indentations seemingly almost drawn in with the pencil. However, if they are secure in understanding that they really can explore the material in an open ended way they will begin to research it practically, play with it, and begin to build up a vocabulary of the characteristics and potential of the medium.

Some children will hardly use their visual faculties at all; though clearly working hard, pushing, pulling, flattening, elongating, squeezing, they will be looking dreamily (or otherwise) elsewhere. Some teachers have found that to invite children to work blindfold at this stage is a very positive experience. This can be undertaken right through the age range, with encouragement after the early exploration, when vision is restored, to form the clay into a shape which felt pleasing to hold, or to help it into something it reminds them of. This challenge should not be introduced too soon, and will not be once we realise that the educational importance lies in the process rather than the product.

It is easy to gauge when genuine exploration is about to degenerate into something less fruitful and to introduce a new challenge, or round off the experience for that day. Respecting concentration spans can be all important in teaching – we all have them! But it is possible to extend them by engaging the children's interests, to sometimes quite surprising lengths.

FORM

Clay exploration which ended as an elephant. Boy, 4 years

Children enjoying handling clay

Mandarin drake. After a visit to a wildlife park. Clay and powder colour. Boy, 6 years

Clay exploration - 'A fast car' and 'Lady in a bath' 7 years

Red deer. After a visit to a park. Twigs which were likened to antlers were brought back.

Coiled figures. After museum visit

Beast

Drawings of the 'Beast'

CONKERS (p.81)

Clay exploration

Joined pinch pots printed and indented

Conker drawings

Conkers

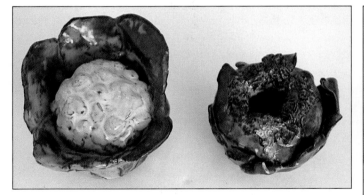

Vegetables

Pinch pot and modelled form based on 'movement' theme

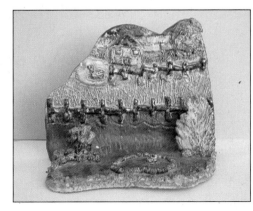

View from the classroom window

The more teachers work in this exploratory way, the more confidence they will have in knowing that children quite spontaneously feel and look at the clay form, and find that it often does remind them of something. This is the same human characteristic young children bring to bear when scribble is 'identified' as a particular named thing. We as adults should understand this concept from our own experience and can look to a long tradition of named rock formations, for example The Old Man, Bowerman's Nose, or the Witch of Wookey. It is reported too, that Leonardo da Vinci was sometimes inspired by looking at the configurations of damp patches on the walls.

This intuitive 'energised by materials' way of working can continue throughout this age range – and much further. If you experiment with a piece of clay yourself, tuning in to feeling and touch rather than sight, you will know that after a period of uncertainty the ideas will often begin to flow and take shape, almost in spite of your preconceptions. The outcomes may be figurative or abstract in form. It may well have something to do with tuning in to less-used sensory experience, or a particular practical involvement moving us toward a more intuitive way of working. The model of the elephant can be seen in this context, and many more examples could be cited. A piece of clay squeezed in one hand by one six-year-old became a racing car, after which a series was made, each with variations and developments. Others include 'A flying bird', 'A dragon', 'A man's head', 'A cave', 'A cross person's head' and so on.

As the children become more experienced the skills and techniques can be built up - pinching, coiling, slabbing, imprinting and modelling in the round and in relief. These are valuable educational practices, which are important in their own right, whether it is possible to fire the outcomes or not. To be able to fire ceramic forms rounds off a wonderful experience and offers insight into the making of so many of the world's artifacts. The dense self-hardening clays are a poor substitute for the natural substance - a truth which can be easily experienced by handling the two materials.

Developments in ceramic sculpture, pottery or modelling can go side by side, and the world of tactile forms can be enriched by displays which can include natural and made items - stones, shells, eggs, wood, bark, bowls, plates, vessels, sculptured and modelled forms, functional containers - all of which can prove to be a rich educational resource.

It is very important to consider light sources when displaying three-dimensional resource material or children's work, as shadow can play a large part in the way we see, understand and enjoy the items displayed. To place an item on a banding wheel, or even a cake turntable, while shining a light from one angle, can be a very interesting experience. This can prove even more dramatic if lights are turned out on a winter afternoon, or blackout is available. Stage or spotlights can be used, but even a large torch or bicycle lamp can be effective. Work can also be explored by touch - and form, weight, surface, texture and temperature can be considered.

The challenge for young children sometimes to make drawings of the models they have made is a good way to relate two- and three-dimensional work. In the long run children can use drawing techniques and researches to plan three-dimensional art and design forms in a positive way, but it must always be remembered that if we challenge them to do so before they have a practical understanding of the material and its characteristics, it is only too easy for them to miss the real strength and potential inherent in it. The practice of designing and making three-dimensional forms by means of materials exploration and maquettes is not uncommon among adult artists and craftspeople and is a sound way of working with children. This approach, together with all the techniques of sensory researching, drawing and diagramming can prove to be the most invaluable tool in many contexts.

EXPERIENCE OF FORM: conkers
Middle school
(9 - 10 years)

The sequence of work leading to the ceramic studies of horse chestnuts began with the children exploring texture by touch, making rubbings, using wax crayons and ink flooding, and building up overlays using tissue and other papers.

Potatoes, onions, stones and ovoid shapes were passed around, and the 'feel' and shape were discussed. Clay was introduced and the children made hollow shapes by joining two pinch pots together. Provided at this stage the air is trapped inside, they can be imprinted and impressed with found objects, twigs and tools, and the shape changed by tapping on the table, or squeezing with the hands (an air hole should be introduced before firing). Textures were worked on, and the cone shapes glazed, using iron, manganese, cobalt and copper. This was painted on thinly and wiped off. Following this process the conkers were studied and felt, and the children were invited to make a three-dimensional 'drawing' in clay. Some of them chose to make two-dimensional drawings in pastels.

SEATED FIGURES
Middle school

Following a life drawing session, I posed for the children in sitting positions. The project then began with the study of pictures of 18th century Staffordshire pew groups, together with some modern pieces which incorporated sitting figures.

The children discussed character, posture, and the stories which might lie behind the little groupings. They were then invited to make one of their own, choosing any kind of seating, and introducing two figures. Slabwork, coiling and modelling could be incorporated and used in any way the children wished. The models were fired, using either oxide and transparent glaze, or white glaze and coloured enamels.

BOXES
A design project
Primary school

The children from a class of 8 - 9 year olds visited the primary base at Anglia Polytechnic University and for a day the whole class worked on the project alongside two tutors and the class teacher. Previously the children had experienced some observational drawing, painting, print making and work with clay.

1 The work

The aims of the project were:

- to explore with a partner the mark-making potential of a range of graphic materials.
- to use 'nets' to make a series of boxes using the resulting piece of decorated paper.

The materials were set out in advance - one piece of A2 cartridge paper between two children and a range of mark-making materials: wax crayons, aquarelle crayons, felt tip pens, 'brusho' or coloured ink, chalk and oil pastels.

The children were asked to choose a partner to work with. They were to have a 'conversation' on the A2 sheet of paper using all or some of the graphic materials provided. Different types of conversation were discussed, for example an argument, a friendly chat, a gossip, a conversation about feelings or a particular mood. The children were asked to think about ways in which their conversation might affect their choice of materials or the marks they would make in response to each other.

We discussed the etiquette of conversation - that it is usual to wait until one person has finished speaking before the other replies, because if two people talk at once it is difficult to hear what the other person is saying, but that it is sometimes permissible to interrupt politely. It was suggested that these conventions of conversation should be borne in mind during their 'conversation' with graphic materials. It was also pointed out that communication would be through the type of mark made in response to each other and not through

PEW GROUPS

Seated figures, based on 18th century Staffordshire pew groups

Musicians

Children work in pairs, patterning the 'conversation' in marks

Cutting and making the boxes

Patterned paper and net-shaped holes

Boxes and nets

normal conversation. This should therefore be a quiet, focused activity. The role of the tutors and teacher was to circulate amongst the children, observing and encouraging them when appropriate to think of ways in which the 'conversation' could develop.

There comes a time in the process when the conversation ends and the resulting marks can be discussed in their own right. The children were shown how to evaluate the mark-making by viewing selected areas through a 'window' torn or cut in a small piece of paper, and then discussing ways of developing the design by working into the spaces or into or over the top of existing marks.

At this stage the children were given a number of nets from which to make boxes. It would have been better if before the mark-making the children had explored in maths the concept of the nets of boxes and had experimented on squared paper devising their own, or had collapsed existing small boxes to discover a variety of nets, and so be in a position to make choices about which net to use. Unfortunately as time was limited this was not possible. It was suggested that if the net was cut out carefully, the net-shaped hole which was left could be used as a window through which to identify the best position of the template. Holding the net firmly, it was then drawn round. In some cases it was necessary to use a black felt tip pen for this so that the line showed over the pattern. Care was needed when marking the flaps. The nets were then folded and the flaps glued to make a box.

2 Value

This is a design-related project with many starting points, making it appropriate to a wide age range. It also has much potential for cross-curricular work.

3 Further developments

This project has potential for alternative starting points and extension activities. The paper from which the boxes are made could be designed to relate to a specific class topic or personal enthusiasm, and could be printed instead of being an area for the exploration of graphic materials. Extension activities could be of a cross-curricular nature - for example in maths the nets of other three-dimensional shapes could be investigated. A selection of these shapes could then be combined to form a sculpture. The sculpture itself is then quite a challenge to draw, particularly if surface pattern is taken into account. The boxes could also act as a stimulus for language work as they could contain a related message, poem or story. Alternatively the boxes could be filled with a variety of dry materials and weighed. Nor is it only a suitable activity for juniors, as one class of Year 1 children found out. They chose a partner, patterned a sheet of paper between them and used this paper to make boxes. They tested the boxes for stress and were very surprised to find that they withstood a pressure of 640 gm. This was equivalent to 4 large cooking apples weighing 1lb 6oz.

COLOUR

'She learned the difference that form could make to colour, but she saw no reason why colour in its abstract analogies with human emotion should be restricted by shape at all, except in so far as it required area and space. The responses of her children had helped to teach her that ...'

Christopher Neve on the points of view of Winifred Nicholson,
Unknown Colour, Faber, 1987.

Colour is one of the key elements in art and design, and one which can be much enhanced and developed by sensitive teaching. The full experience of colour is a fundamental one which influences and affects the majority of our children, with some exceptions for those who have some impairment, restricted colour vision, partial sight or blindness. It is of course important to diagnose children in these categories in order to offer appropriate experience. Other than with total blindness colour can play a positive part, and can be enjoyed and used to good effect.

First-hand experience of colour lies at the heart of the matter; children must be made aware of its potential, and the rewarding quality of seeing must be given full reign, as well as the freedom to use pigments and materials. It is possible if the subject is taught in a particular technical manner that it can be 'analysed to bits', losing all the vigour and interest which can entice children to real depths of interest in its qualities, pleasures and uses.

It is a fallacy to think that children must understand the mechanics, properties and so-called rules of colour behaviour and mixing before being able to use it with power and subtlety. Our youngest children will often confound us by their strong, immediate, intuitive work - provided they have been given the materials and tools. This is not an argument against overt teaching and the expansion and development of colour practice, with all the technical nuances appropriate to the child's understanding, but it is important to make sure that the work is always seen in the context of a living experience. Much colour teaching will have cross-curricular potential not only in art and design context, but also in descriptive and creative language usage, in humanities, and in science.

From early years children have been surrounded by the natural and made environment. Colour experience and the language pertaining to it will be built up steadily by teachers who are aware of the educational value of this vibrant means of understanding and response, and who know its full descriptive, communicative and expressive potential.

Materials and tools

It is very important to see that the materials and tools that children are presented with are appropriate, of sound quality, and rewarding to handle. Classroom resources and collections of all kinds should be rich in a broad range of colour items, and will prove very fruitful educationally. A basic range of good quality paint is a crucial necessity to enable colour mixing experience, and it is a waste of teacher and pupil time and energy if an appropriate range is not available. It is of the utmost importance to keep a careful watch on stocks of basic colours in order not to run out. There will be times when teachers decide to challenge

COLOUR EXPERIMENTATION

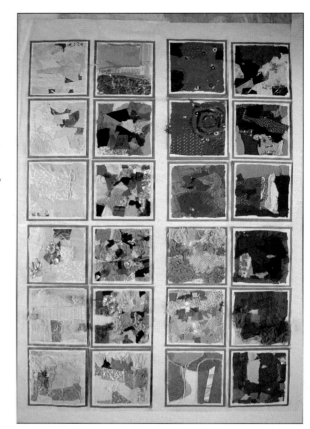

Nursery children experimenting with colour and print with toy car wheels

Mixed media collage and watercolour inks. Boy, 9 years

Every child in the class was challenged to make a unit based on a primary or secondary colour. Each unit 22 cm sq. 7-8 years

Each child was asked to wrap wools of a particular colour range round a strip of mounting board offcut. 9-10 years

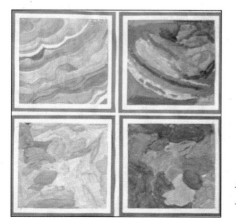

Mixing and matching. Powder colour. 7-8 years

Snow and winter. Collage. Units 27 x 16 cm. The children were asked to make collage rectangles on this theme, for mounting as a group panel

Responding to paint. 'Big face'. 4 years. 51 x 63 cm. Paint mixed by the teacher. Children often go through a stage of using non-representational colour

Responding to oil pastels. 'Window'. Girl, 6 years. 51 x 63 cm. Oil pastels are excellent in their own right, and can also help children who have difficulty exerting pressure.

Responding to paint. 'Pattern'. Girl, 7 years. 41 x 59 cm. One of a series of patterns Laura undertook. All are strong shaped and varied in hue and pattern.

yellow and blue made green.

red and yellow made orange

red and blue made purple

kirsty

First attempts at colour mixing. Kirsty, 5 years. 54 x 25.5 cm. The teacher has talked to her and labelled what has happened

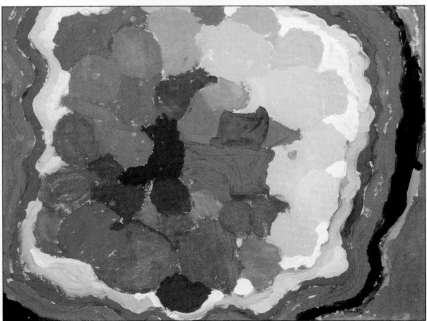

Colour mixing game. Tempera colour. Three children were asked to mix colours and group them in families. They chose to surround their efforts with circles of colour

children to use a limited palette, but this will be for educational reasons rather than necessity. (It is a useful rule of thumb to order twice as much yellow and white paint as the other colours; they will generally be used in larger amounts.)

Paint should be of the kind which can be mixed to a thick, creamy consistency, and the hues should be strong and clear. Powder colour or ready-mixed varieties of tempera or acrylic all have much to offer, and have different qualities.

Powder colour is a good general-use paint. It can be used thickly and has excellent covering potential and opacity. It is easy to store and organise, and children can be taught to handle and mix it for themselves at a very early age. Few classrooms would be without it. It is not good when used as a wash, or transparent medium; it becomes gritty and loses the quality of the hue when it is watered down. The viscosity can be changed by the addition of a PVA adhesive, a squeeze of a thick washing up liquid, or a polycell base (the latter is inclined to thin the paint).

Tempera. Ready-mixed paints are very useful and respond well to being used thickly, or as a transparent medium.

Acrylic polymer paints are also available, and are very versatile. They have excellent adhesive properties and can be used thickly, with PVA added, or transparently with water. They can be used for painting or printmaking.

There is a case to be made for schools to carry a basic stock of powder colour, together with some stocks of the other two paints for particular needs. The basic range should include black, white, and a cold and warm hue of each of the primary colours - red, yellow and blue. Greens, purples and oranges are not really necessary as the basic range used skilfully should make these mixtures possible (though of course you may sometimes need a particular additional colour).

Adequate non-tip stacking water pots, mixing palettes and a range of good quality brushes are also an absolute necessity (there are many plastic food containers with at least a 500 g capacity which are ideal for water. It is useful for children to have two each).

As children work practically, and learn in their environment, the teacher will no doubt introduce the naming of colours in the context of a whole package of exploration and experiment, supported by looking, searching, selecting and sorting in as many different guises as can be devised.

Colour displays and exhibitions can also play a useful role, and very often children show great surprise that there are so many variations of a single hue.

From initial 'family' naming, and practical grouping - reds, blues, yellows, purples, greens, oranges, browns, greys, blacks, whites, for example, language experience can be developed and children can be encouraged to use subtle descriptions and extend their vocabulary. Very often children respond by describing particular colours as 'light' or 'dark' - which is an interesting first stage in differentiating, but is of limited communicative value. The language can be extended by matching known items to a colour - primrose, daffodil yellow, mustard, lemon, brass, gold, for example, all conjure up specific hues which are easily pictured in the mind. This was a favourite method used by the painter Winifred Nicholson when she was talking to students, and one which very few people ever forgot.

Collections of decorators' colour charts and collage material can add greatly to the school or classroom 'bank', together with natural items from the environment. Art and design forms - paintings, drawings, sculpture, textiles and prints, together with reproductions of all kinds - will complete this valuable teaching resource. The whole experience of colour awareness can quite naturally grow alongside direct practical work.

Evidence of the effectiveness of the teaching strategies will become apparent in the outcomes of further direct challenges, or in colour practice generally.

Usage - Exploration - Experimentation - Usage - is a cycle of experience which should continue throughout the child's art and design education.

Usage	Children's own communicative and expressive drives - painting, collage, textiles, and sculptural work in school. Colour work in other contexts and subject areas. Response to a variety of challenges.
Exploration	Finding out about the qualities and the nature of things by experience. Mixing - using different pigments with different tools. Grouping different items. Attaching different items, overlaying items.
Experimentation	'What happens if I do this? How can I make that? How can I make this work?' Mixing, matching, finding particular effects. Answering particular technical and expressive problems.

The colour exemplars

The first part of this section is made up of a number of different explorations and experiments undertaken by children aged 3 - 12. These are followed by a series of projects in schools where the predominant element is colour. (They will also, by the very nature of art and design experience, in part consist of other elements, although clearly not in full in each project or piece of work.) The criteria for including the examples has been the visual evidence of the value of the colour experience. Is it rich and self rewarding? (If it is not there will need to be questions as to whether the materials supplied were at fault, or whether the challenge was appropriate. Colour should not only connect with the intellect - it should reach the heart and solar plexus as well!) Is there real evidence of learning? Is there evidence of understanding which could change future practice? The work can also be assessed from a number of other curricular aspects. Can we find evidence of exploration, experimentation, imagining, observing, recording, beginning to make connections, the development of ideas, and the application of knowledge? The work, and our knowledge of the ways in which the children have approached it, will be the ground on which to base our conclusions.

COLOUR: MEMORY AND IMAGINATION

Christmas robin. Powder paint. 5 years.

Blue bird table. Memory. A painting after looking through coloured cellophanes and gells.

Panji and the buffalo (Javanese folk tale).
Wax resist

King Midas.
Girl , 12 years

Milk for the cat. Girl, 12 years. Partially sighted

COLOUR PROJECT: WATER. Special school

The project included direct experience of looking at water, particularly the River Thames. The children also enjoyed looking at the paintings of Claude Monet on the theme of water.

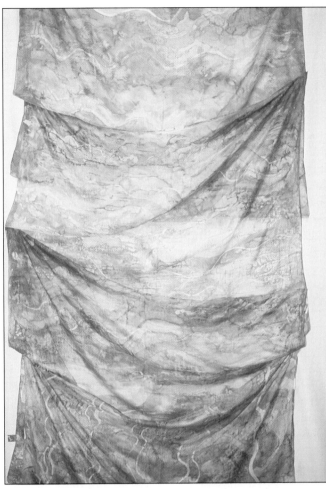

A collection of scarves one metre square.
Dye painted on silk

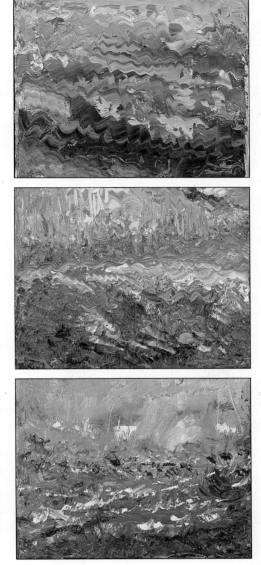

Paintings. Oil on canvas

COLOUR EXPERIENCE Middle schools

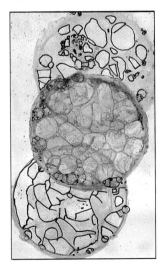

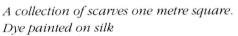

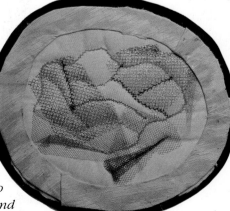

Bubble prints (pigment and washing up liquid) built up, drawn and drawn into. These prints were developed using nets and embroidered

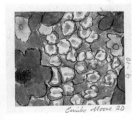

Miniature paintings. Girl. 10 years

COLOUR: Houses and homes: batik

11 children aged 9 years.

An artist in schools project

Shaheen Merali in a Special School for delicate children

The project was set up by the London Borough of Enfield, using a funding grant from Greater London Arts Association. It involved artists from Panchayat, a group dedicated to exploring art in a multicultural context within different schools and environments. The project involved the whole class for one day a week. Although Shaheen Merali led the project and directed the children, the class teacher and a welfare assistant were present to assist where necessary. The art teacher worked in partnership with the artist, coordinating and liaising during the project and was present as support for part of the day.

1 Background

This is a special school for emotionally and physically delicate children. It caters for children with a multiplicity of special needs. Although the average age of the class was 9 years, one must look further than their chronological age when considering their levels of understanding, ability and performance. One of the major educational aims for all the staff in the school is to extend the children's experience in every possible way, in order to maximise the potential and ability of every child. The short concentration span of some pupils is a continual challenge, as is the build up of listening skills and the ability to follow simple instructions.

The children have used a variety of graphic tools, paint, clay and collage. They have worked from direct observation as well as undertaking imaginative work.

2 The work

We found that to have the stimulus of an artist in school was an exciting event for pupils and staff. It proved to be a learning experience from which all participants as well as others in the school benefited. In order to maximise the effectiveness of the project, the school and artist have to be suitably matched, and the initial planning and discussion stages very carefully undertaken in order to align expectations and practicalities.

The planning of every stage of the activity and the siting of materials and equipment was most important. The help of the caretaker was enlisted to rearrange the furniture for each session. In the middle of the room was a block of tables that could be used for drawing, wax application and ironing. The dyes, having been mixed by Shaheen and the children, were arranged at the back of the room.

Shaheen Merali, an artist who has moved from sculpture to installations, and now works in a variety of media, was able to share his immense wealth of experience and expertise as artist and educator, in stimulating and motivating the class. The project was designed to target multicultural art in school and extend the children's ideas and experiences by considering new ways of working.

The topic 'Houses and homes' had already been decided upon earlier at primary curriculum planning meetings. Shaheen was happy to work to this remit, discussing his ideas with staff and involving the children at every stage. Batik (wax resist) painting was the chosen medium, and it was Shaheen's suggestion that each child should complete a panel measuring about 50 x 50 cm. We had the luxury of using real silk together with exquisitely vibrant dyes. These, together with large sheets of white sugar paper, some smaller pieces of drawing paper, a batik pot for heating the wax, 4B pencils and some old paint brushes, completed the needs for our venture.

The project included learning about the skills, techniques and history of batik. Drawing from observation led to selecting designs to compose a pleasing composition. The designs were then executed using hot wax and dyestuffs. The children's enthusiasm was sustained throughout the whole six weeks, which was mainly due to the artist and staff planning for progression and continuity that built upon success. By engaging in a constant dialogue about what was happening, or about to happen, the children were able to understand and appreciate each stage. The day was broken into four parts, two in the morning with a mid-morning break and two after lunch, also with a break. As the children had never done any batik work before, each session was full of exciting challenges, and their concentration spans remained surprisingly long. We introduced music from different parts of the world, and talked about customs and cultures. Work was undertaken both in and out of school and the focus changed from art, through geography, history, creative story telling and maths.

3 Sequence of working

The initial discussion about homes and buildings led to drawing buildings, both outside from direct observation, and in the classroom using other visual resources. The first drawing exercise took place in the classroom and was designed to encourage them to observe carefully. In pairs, they had to think about drawing each other, to close their eyes and feel their partner's face, then draw what they had felt. This exercise provoked much discussion. The children decided that it was much easier, and produced better results, if you drew with eyes open! But the purpose had been fulfilled. The experience helped them to focus more fully when they drew their partner's face, concentrating wonderfully on all those details that they may previously have taken for granted.

The same level of concentrated observational work was apparent the following week when they drew self portraits using mirrors. The pupils were also given the opportunity to dress up in clothes, fabrics and headgear from different parts of the world. We mixed scarves and sarees with protective helmets and Muslim skull caps. We used Ikat woven sarongs from Indonesia and patterned cloth from India. We followed this experience by working outside in the playground, making drawings of the surrounding school buildings and houses and found the level of observation and care in the execution of the task quite astounding.

The last session of the day took place back in the classroom. The children had access to a large selection of photographs and reproductions of buildings which fulfilled different purposes - including temples, mosques and churches. There were also examples of the work of architects, and different kinds of paintings, prints and drawings.

At the end of the first day each child had a number of completed drawings, consisting of buildings and people. These were to form the basis of the composition for the batik.

We enlarged the children's drawings on the photocopier. Some were duplicated, allowing for repeat patterns. The final design was to be the same size

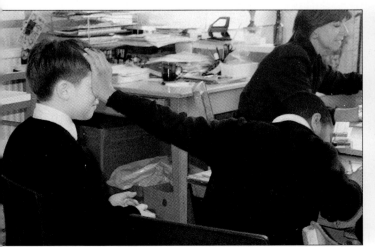 

Drawing, using books and reproductions

Cutting out the enlarged designs

Rearranging the components

Final touches to the drawing

Painting dye onto the waxed cloth

Time for evaluation

Final panel design. Drawn, enlarged, cut out and rearranged

Batik panel relating to design

Batik panels. 50 x 50 cm

as the rectangle of silk. The children cut out their drawings, repositioning them on backing paper until they were satisfied with the composition. The designs were then traced onto the cloth using a fine line spirit-based indelible pen. Both the paper and the cloth need to be anchored to the table with masking tape, stretching the cloth taught. Tracing had to be done quickly and lightly, to prevent the ink spreading onto the silk. The panels were also used as inspiration for creative writing, each child being encouraged to describe what was happening in their picture. These stories were finally displayed with the designs. Drawing superfluous to their immediate needs for the batiks were used as a group composition for a classroom frieze. At this point we were ready to undertake the waxing, and the purpose-made electric 'batik pot' was introduced and the techniques explained, with the importance of safety and correct procedure strongly emphasised. The line designs were waxed over using a paintbrush, ensuring that enough wax had been applied to maintain a barrier between the colours and act as a resistant edge for the dyes. Sometimes it was found necessary to wax on both sides of the line. Every child carried out the waxing and dyeing process competently and safely, with assistance only when necessary.

Following the first waxing process it had been decided that the pale colour dyes should be applied first, so that the later applications of wax and stronger colours could interact and overlay them. The second waxing was applied over the pale colours to add pattern and texture. The final colours used were rich and strong.

The wax was removed from the cloth by ironing. Layers of newsprint were placed under the batik and on top, in order to absorb the melted wax. The paper needs to be changed frequently so that all the wax is removed. The colours and patterns are now seen for the first time in their full splendour. (The pieces can also be dry cleaned to remove the final traces of wax.)

The children were continually assessing their work, making decisions and judgements about colour, pattern, texture, line and shape. The level of their participation and ambition to succeed was evident and the finished panels reflect a high level of enjoyment and involvement.

'Houses and homes' was used as a starting point for other cross-curricular work. Historical and geographical aspects formed a natural part of the discussion, and any of the themes could have been further extended. The mathematical problem of costing out each finished piece was a fascinating exercise, and one which revealed much more than a final sum of money. It provoked discussion about valuing one's work, about it being valued by others, as well as what it means to be an artist. Preparing and displaying work for public exhibition proved to be very exciting.

4 Value

There are many underlying and less obvious benefits from working with an artist in school. The children enjoyed having another adult in the class, and the sharing of the expertise and skills of the class teacher, the art teacher and the artist helped foster a mutual confidence and understanding. The class responded well to the multicultural focus of the project. It gave the opportunity for discussion about clothing, customs, ceremonies and celebrations. Music, mainly from India, was played during some of the sessions. Shaheen proved to be a very positive role model for the black and Asian children in the class. It was the festival of Eid at the time, which actively involved two members of the class; this provide another rich topic for discussion.

The project has definitely raised the awareness of other pupils and staff throughout the school, which has undoubtedly enhanced the children's concentration, motivation and self-esteem. One pupil whose self-image was usually a problem, and whose continual cry was that his own work was 'rubbish', or that he could not do it, responded in this instance by a thoughtful silence followed by the remark 'Oh Miss - it's beautiful!' The headteacher gave her full support to the whole venture, and visitors seemed to appear at every session to watch the work in progress. The children were keen throughout, and very confident when discussing their progress or exhibiting their work.

5 Possible developments

In retrospect it could be seen that the restricted timescale meant that some opportunities that arise from such an event may have been missed. The project proved to be a sound incentive and motivation from which more work could be undertaken. The creative writing could have been extended to include poems, drama and more stories. The whole project could have been written up as a diary, recording the events and processes. These could have been accompanied by drawings or the many photographs taken. It would have been most useful to the school, and others wishing to pursue the same project, to video the different stages and aspects of the project. The theme could be developed in paint, collage, drawing and modelling of all kinds. Colour and pattern could be further explored; this would have been a natural extension of looking at the patterned fabrics.

The panels were exhibited at a local department store and also at the teachers professional development centre. The pupils were very excited at seeing their work on display. The acknowledgement of their achievements, by themselves and by others, was a vital part of the learning that took place. The panels are a permanent testimonial to the success of such a project, but they are only the tip of the iceberg as to what happened educationally. The level of enjoyment and understanding has had benefits and left memories that will be long lasting and far-reaching.

COLOUR: autumn term curriculum work
11 - 12 years

The work here shows some examples of curriculum practice which have been firmly rooted in the activities of investigating, making and understanding. The visual language of art is taught through practical handling of tools and materials, encouragement to become involved and to look, and through the study of all kinds of art and design forms. Experience in the elements of art is steadily built up. This particular work is very strongly orientated toward colour, but shape, pattern, texture and line also play an important part. Sketchbooks have been used as a means of investigating natural and made forms, and in finding out about the way in which artists have worked. They are also used for brainstorming, working on imaginative ideas and for all kinds of designing.

When we make studies of pictures they are never merely copied: there is always something to be found out about the colour, subject matter, composition, or the general atmosphere of the piece of work. The children are encouraged to think for themselves and to look at the means by which effects have been achieved. The strength of a good curriculum should lie in the fact that the skills and approaches which have been assimilated are transferable, and can be built on in other contexts.

Language experience plays a powerful part in the work, and there is a wholeness of approach which can be a natural stimulus to both disciplines.

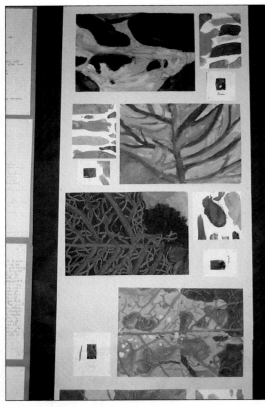

Framed leaf fragments and colour notes

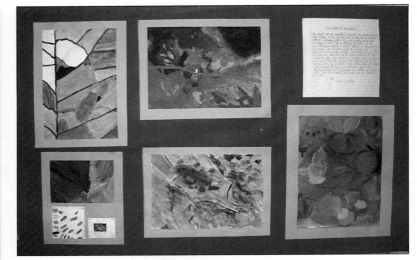

Paintings. Sections of leaves

Dyed background with pastel drawing

Dyed background with printed motif, drawn into with pastel

Dyed background with pastel drawing

Following study of Arcimboldo's seasonal face paintings, and reading an extract from Kafka's metamorphosis, art and language work was developed

Classroom display panel on the theme of change (Arcimboldo in top centre)

Autumn portrait, influenced by Arcimboldo's heads

Collaged head

Analysing colour from reproductions of artists' work

Single section books and sketchbooks

COLOUR: FOLK TALES

1 Background and previous experience

An Artist in Schools Project
Rebecca Price in a First and Middle School

I read reports of the artist in schools scheme and thought, 'If these schools can have an artist, why can't we?' I made enquiries and followed them up by an approach to our regional association, South East Arts, to apply for funding. We were successful.

We thought carefully about the kind of artist we would like to have, and discussed it with the South East Arts Artists in Schools Scheme representative. It was felt that art was traditionally not one of the stronger subjects in the school, and there was a general consensus that it was a curriculum area which needed a real boost. When specifically thinking about our needs, a number of points were raised:

1 The project should benefit all the children, not just a few.

2 It had to be attainable as an experience to everyone.

3 It had to be something which would continue to affect the children and us after the artist went away.

On looking at the practice in the school it seemed that the four, five and six year olds enjoyed using paint confidently, exploring and experimenting with brushes and premixed powder colours. Later, drawing experience using pencils, charcoal and pastels seemed to take over, and the painting, which many children now did not like, seemed to become trapped in a drawn structure. It almost developed into an exercise in 'filling in', with the children becoming frustrated, feeling that the drawings were being spoilt by the paint. The drawing activities were of interest in their own right, and quite a lot of work was based on first-hand experience and looking; but in the words of a member of staff, it stopped there.

We had some experience of showing children original works, as we belonged to an LEA loan scheme.

On negotiating with South East Arts and considering a number of artists, Rebecca Price seemed to be the very person we were looking for, with her strong vibrant use of colour. She agreed to come and spend the mornings helping children with ideas and practical work, and afternoons undertaking her own painting in a situation where children could see her at work and talk about it to her.

This was agreed, and arrangements made in school:

a for her own work to be displayed

b to enable her to paint in the craft room where the children could watch

c for the children to be timetabled in groups of eight to spend a whole morning working with her

d for classes of children to be timetabled to watch Rebecca working on her paintings and have the opportunity to question her

e for a staff painting workshop after school one day

f for upper and lower school assemblies where Rebecca could exhibit her work and talk to the children. This was in fact a great success. The children filed into the hall, and gasped at the impact of colour in these large pieces of work. Rebecca put on her painting smock and introduced them to her tools and materials. She showed them slides of her childhood work and talked about it and told them what she was interested in, leading them to her recent work, and her interest in folk tales. The children's response was very positive, and there was a high level of involved and excited discussing and questioning.

2 Report on the scheme by the artist, Rebecca Price

My Work

Since completing my studies at the Slade School of Fine Art in 1988, I have shown paintings regularly in solo and group shows in London, Newcastle, Bath, Leicester, Peterborough, Maidstone and Los Angeles. Some of the work I produced during the residency was included in a solo exhibition later in the year. Taking part in a school residency was something I had wanted to do for a long time, as a way of extending and sharing my experience.

My paintings are mainly concerned with colour relationships, which I use to develop my ideas. After making a small study of what I intend to do I start working straight on to the canvas. As I use oil paint, I can change the colours and shapes numerous times before finally consolidating them. I wanted to encourage the children to work on a painting over an extended period, helping them to change it until the colours reacted in relation to the subject matter.

The workshops

The residency took place for two days a week over a period of five weeks. Although the children were working with me for three hours on each occasion, none of them lost concentration and some begged to continue into the afternoon.

My recent paintings had been about folk tales, so I decided to use these as the subject matter. Each child had a table and I arranged them in a ring around where I was working. I laid out powder paints, palettes already filled with washing-up-liquid as a medium for the paint, a variety of brushes and a palette knife. At first I gave them sugar paper to paint on but soon changed this to card, as the paper proved to be too flexible, and the thick paint cracked as it dried.

I read the selected stories to each age group as they sat around me and then focused on the idea from the story. They then began working, usually in absorbed silence. I worked on my own painting and went round to help them from time to time. No-one asked to draw in pencil first, and composition was never a problem: the main subject always filled the page, but initially I did find that each child needed to be shown how to mix the paint thickly enough.

Halfway through the morning, I showed postcards of relevant work by important artists. The children chose favourite and least favourite images, often disagreeing with each other but discussing them thoroughly. The younger children liked images as diverse as Van Goch, Turkish miniatures, Vermeer and Warhol. Rembrandt was not popular: 'Too dark'. Older children preferred more recent artists such as Kandinsky, Monet, Picasso and Derain, particularly the bold and often unrepresentational uses of colour.

At one point in the postcard session, havoc broke out when one six-year-old was found writing on the back of a postcard. Next moment the whole lot had been turned over and private messages to myself were being read out in steady 'learning to read' voices. It was with some trouble that I managed to restore interest to the front of the postcards again! After seeing the postcards, the children's ideas always became more focused and the colours got cleaner.

To the youngest (age 5 - 6 years) I read 'The Princess and the Pea'. After reading the story, I told them to shut their eyes and imagine the pile of mattresses and quilts towering up to the ceiling.

'What colours can you see?'

Various colours were named, although one little boy complained that he couldn't see any mattresses, only blackness .... Happily the others argued that they had indeed seen plenty of mattresses.

I showed them a collection of fabrics as a resource stimulus, and after handling them they decided which might have been suitable for quilts. Dark red velvet proved the unanimous favourite, after much stroking.

Painting the pile of mattresses was pictorially simple enough for them to concentrate on mixing paint, without getting distracted by extra detail. They considered colour juxtaposition and enjoyed using palette knives on black paper.

FOLK TALES

1 'Away he went, over stock and stone, until his hair whistled in the wind.' Rebecca Price. 165 x 165 cm

2 'Ripe strawberries which came up quite red out of the snow' Rebecca Price. 165x 165 cm

3-4 The pile of mattresses. From 'The Princess and the pea'. 5-6 years

5 Trying on the paper dress

6 Maid Maleen's dark cave. 8-9 years

7 *Children try on the prince's hats, from 'The Golden Bird'*

8 *The sunshade. 10-11 years*

9, 10, 11 *The thicket, from 'Little Briar Rose'. 11 years*

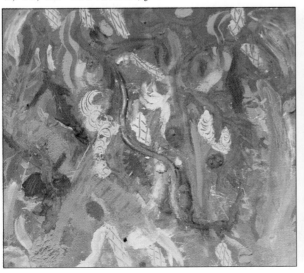

They all loved mixing paint for the first time, always relating it to food: 'My water looks like milk shake.' 'Mine looks like hot chocolate.' 'This is a peachy colour.'

I found that using props such as the pieces of material proved very useful, so I introduced further resources. One group tried on hats, to imagine which the prince in the story might have worn. I made a paper dress for one group to try on, so that they could identify with the girl who was sent out into the snow in such a garment. One little boy was particularly eager to try it on: I was pleased about this because it showed that both boys and girls could identify with the story. Imagining that they were the hero or heroine of a story encouraged the children to incorporate their own ideas and emotions into their paintings.

I introduced umbrellas and mirrors for a story about a magic parasol, under which a person was made to look more beautiful. This group of 10 - 11-year-olds were encouraged to start using their own reflected faces to solve drawing problems and also to paint the umbrellas from first hand experience.

'Maid Maleen' is a story about a girl who is locked up in a completely dark tower for seven years before escaping. With a group of eight to nine year olds I focused on her release into the brightly coloured sunshine. They produced quite abstract work, where areas of dark colour contrasted with bright ones.

The oldest group (11 - 12 years) did paintings of the forest scene from 'Little Briar Rose' (similar to 'The Sleeping Beauty'). After showing them reproductions of Abstract Expressionists, in particular Jackson Pollock, they experimented energetically with textures to represent the density and gloom of the forest. They enjoyed working on ideas which were not constrained by the need for figuration.

My own work during the residency

The afternoons were set aside for my own work. I began seven new paintings and completed two. The groups were brought in to watch in silence as I worked and then given the opportunity to ask questions. I usually spend much of my time thinking about the painting I am working on, but with thirty eagerly expectant children watching me, I could hardly sit and think the whole time, so I found myself putting on far more paint in a less considered way than usual, and having to alter it later when I had time to make better decisions.

The most interesting and intelligent questions often came from the children whom I later discovered to be the most troublesome in class! The younger children could always see what my semi-abstract paintings depicted, while their teachers stood by, baffled. This would lead to discussion about whether a painting needs to be figurative; I asked the children if a painting could be about something other than real things. One five-year-old impressively volunteered that 'it could just be about colour.'

In addition to the workshops I gave a slide show and talked to the whole school, and also ran an evening for the teachers to explore paint.

Values and developments of the residency

1 Enthusiasm in the children for art: both in producing pictures and talking about artists' work, both my own and the reproductions.

2 A feeling of success and fulfilment, with the children enjoying expressing themselves through art.

3 A new sense of confidence, especially in children who thought they were 'no good at art' because they thought they couldn't draw: they were encouraged to experiment with colour, texture and non-figurative ideas, and could see from the reproductions I showed them that there are other ways of making art.

4 Using different tools and techniques.

5 One child whose grandfather had just died did a painting in her own class

session about her feelings for him, as a result of seeing one of my own paintings about death.

6 Language development - conversation and lots of creative writing: prose and poems written as a result of looking at my work.

7 Several teachers took up the ideas I was using and continued and developed them with their own classes.

8 For myself it was very interesting working in a new environment. Being in a school again reminded me of many of my own emotions as a child; feelings which I am always striving to incorporate into my work. It was also great after working more or less in solitude to be surrounded by interested faces and treated as some sort of celebrity!

Final word from the co-ordinating art teacher
This residency really was a success in every way, and we have made a strong relationship with Rebecca. The interesting part was that it got better all the time. You couldn't help being interested in the colour, but even some of the people who could not understand the paintings at first changed their way of looking at them and enjoyed them the more they saw them. The children too got more and more deeply involved as it went on. It has had an effect, and I hope we go on developing. There has been a turnover of four members of staff since the residency, so the follow-up cannot be as powerful as we had hoped, but still, they will have gone on to other schools, so they will benefit.

List of stories used
    'The Princess and the Pea' by Hans Anderson

    'The Golden Bird' by the brothers Grimm

    'Maid Maleen' by the brothers Grimm

    'The Three Little Men in the Woods' by the brothers Grimm

    'The Sunshade' by Ferra-Mikura

    'Little Briar Rose' by the brothers Grimm

HOLES, GAPS AND CAVITIES

Following a P.E. session in which the children (9-10 years) explored space and form through their own body movements, a painting challenge was issued.
Interpretations could be literal or abstract, based on visual information and/or feeling.

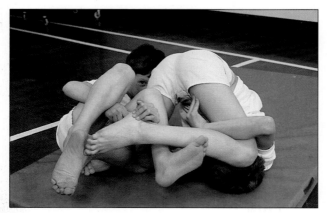

OBSERVATIONAL PAINTING

Primary School. Whole class project. Duration: one afternoon. 10 - 11 years.

1 Previous experience

- observational drawing from wood using twigs dipped in ink
- observational painting from fruit and vegetables

2 The work

Organisation: as working from still life was to be a whole-class event, it was necessary to give careful consideration to structure and organisation. At the end of the morning session the arrangements for the afternoon were discussed and the children given a brief description of the nature of the activity and the range of still life groups from which they would be working. Volunteers were invited to help to re-arrange the furniture. It was explained to the children that when they returned they should wait outside the classroom door where they would be given the opportunity, within reason, to choose where they would like to work. It was also pointed out however that should one particular subject be oversubscribed it would be necessary for them to go without fuss to where there was a space. The children appreciated that this was a special session as in addition to two still-life groups one of the options would be to draw an adult who was going to sit for them. The balance of individual preferences worked very well and the children were quickly in place and ready to begin. Paints, palettes, brushes and water were placed on the tables before the children's arrival and it was explained to them before they began that should they need a change of water or more paint they would need to put up their hand and just for that afternoon they would be waited on.

Objectives

- to create an atmosphere of enthusiasm and provide a rich and varied stimulus
- to encourage the children to observe carefully
- to provide an opportunity for the children to be aware of and to mix colour

Subject matter

Three still-life groups were set up. The first consisted of a group of plants, pots and a lamp on a cloth arranged on a circular table so that the children could sit round it. It presented the problem that there was no given background and there was some discussion as to how this could be solved. The children dealt with this in a variety of ways, as can be seen from the examples shown. The second still life was, by contrast, rich and warm in colour. The mandolin in its case was complemented by the drapes which surrounded it. It was interesting to observe ways in which the design on the red fabric was resolved, one of the most successful solutions being the use of the other end of the brush to draw into the paint. A number of the children were excited by the challenge of the third still life, my mother sitting sewing brightly coloured knitted squares in front of a pastel striped curtain. This was their first attempt at drawing from life. It was suggested to them that they could choose to paint the figure in the context of the environment or select the upper part of the figure and concentrate on portraying the personality of the sitter.

3 Value

Evaluation of the work was encouraged by placing the paintings in white window mounts and displaying them alongside two of the still life groups and photographs of the children working. As the display was located in the school foyer it provoked much discussion not only among peers but also among members of other classes. The children were justifiably proud of their achievements.

4 Further developments

Working in this way with a who[le]
frequent occurrence. It is mo[re]
development from this activity th[at]
select and arrange their own still-li[fe]
'still shot' from an everyday event or [a]
previously performed, and to use that [...]
children are challenged and given oppo[rtunity to]
produce quality work.

THE LOWRY PROJECT

Primary School
Infants 4 - 7 years

A whole school project, which included all the children, members of staff, the secretary, caretaker and some parents.
Time span - 3 weeks.

1 Previous experience

Strongly motivated exploration of materials, and encouragement to paint, draw and model. Working from a variety of bases; careful looking and imaginative work.

Encouragement to think for themselves.

During the previous year, a collection of art books and reproductions had been purchased, and the children had been looking at the work of Van Gogh, Monet, Klimt, and Lowry in particular.

2 The work

The County Art and Design Adviser invited a number of schools (from all age sectors) to take part in a project which entailed planning and carrying out a series of large painted panels. These were to be presented as a section of the Education stand at the Suffolk Show. Each work was to be carried out on a canvas panel (2m x 2m) in acrylic paint, and these materials were supplied.

Each school was to undertake a single panel, which for Whitton Infants happened to be the last in the row, next to the police stand. This fact was carefully considered by the children, and they later put the police into the finished work.

The brief was to communicate some aspects of the work being undertaken in schools where children had already enjoyed responding to and learning from works of art in a practical way.

In order to address this particular challenge, the staff decided that the panel should be based on a townscape by Lowry. The fact that we are in a town on an estate would allow for the content to be based on our surroundings rather than to make a pastiche of the Lowry works.

The staff also decided that it would be a good idea to select a group of children who would enjoy the designing and constructing challenge, and take on the roll of leaders. This seemed preferable to a total involvement by all children in a haphazard way, or teacher-directed composition and arrangement. They realised that there would have to be teacher support throughout, but were anxious that the children did not miss out on the challenge of designing the panel themselves.

(p.108)

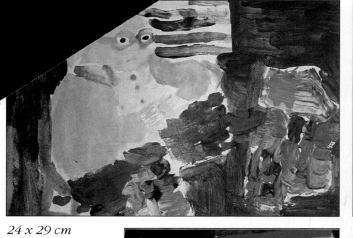

24 x 29 cm

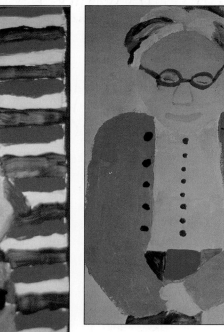

26 x 19 cm

34 x 24cm

23 x 24 cm

STILL LIFE PAINTINGS

Still life with instruments

23 x 35 cm

23 x 35cm

26 x 38 cm

Section of fruit. 25 x 33 cm

Eight children between the ages of 6 - 7 years were invited to join the team - four boys and four girls.

The criteria for the choice of these children was their ability to enjoy working independently, and their enthusiasm and confidence in relation to art.

In the first session the team came together I briefed them about the whole project, their part in it, and the fact that we wanted every single child in the school to play a practical part in the finished piece. The team were taken to the hall and looked at the canvas, paint, mixing palettes, brushes and drawing materials. I then told them about the subject matter, and we began to look at the reproductions of Lowry paintings. I talked about him, where he lived, how he worked, his interests and his life.

The team joined in the discussion enthusiastically, offering their own ideas and questions. What was he trying to do? What was he really interested in? How carefully he must have looked - he must have gone about the streets just looking and drawing. What colours had he seen? What shapes had he drawn in buildings, chimneys, doors, windows? How did he capture character, mood and movement? How did he do it?

They were surprised that when they looked carefully at the figures in his pictures they were not as detailed as they had first supposed.

This initial session, which lasted two hours, really stretched them and they were bubbling with ideas and enthusiasm. The language experience was good, and they were communicating very well, using a much richer vocabulary than usual as they tried to question and describe.

By the second session they had worked out, with teacher support, what they were going to do. The panel needed a basic structure - as Lowry's paintings also had. They decided to have three main areas which were to be defined by two horizontal lines. The top area would be sky, the middle band buildings, and the lower would be ground. The sky would be interestingly shaped because of all the roofs and chimneys. The buildings would be arranged in a row, and would be roughly the same scale. They would be based on the buildings in this particular part of Ipswich. A decision was made to include the police station. Before embarking on the drawing we decided to experiment with the acrylic paint, which we had not used before. It proved a real challenge! Eventually we learned that there was an optimum liquidity which made it a lovely medium to work in. If it was just right it was manageable and had good covering power.

When we had got the feel of the media we set ourselves to mixing the colours for the buildings, making sure that we had mixed sufficient amounts for use. An interesting range of pinks, yellows, buffs and browns were built up and placed together so that the general effect could be considered. These were then put to one side, and the drawing began, using thick pieces of charcoal.

The horizontals were drawn in and surveyed. When they were considered satisfactory the team drew the buildings in the middle band, thinking very carefully about the shape and characteristics of the different structures.

Then the team painted the buildings using the colours they had previously mixed.

On the second day the team worked for an hour. They were divided into two groups, and following appraisal of the work, discussion, and further looking at Lowry paintings, some of them decided on the colour of the sky, while others were attacking the road surface.

On the third day, in a session again lasting about an hour, more colours were mixed, and clouds, paths, street furniture, details of windows and doors, chimneys and smoke were enthusiastically added. The children were constantly encouraged to think of our own area rather than lifting imagery directly from the Lowry works.

The main construction of our scene was set and we were now ready to paint the characters. This was the time for the whole school to be involved. We considered it important that our team should still hold the responsibility as to what was to happen next. They were invited to brief the other children, as they came to take part in the work.

There had been a stream of visitors whilst the initial work went on, and children, staff and parents seemed intrigued to follow the progress, coming into the hall before school, at break, during lunch hours, and at the end of the day.

Over the remaining two weeks it was a matter of snatching time when we could to complete the work. The team was broken down into twos or threes, taking turns to brief groups of twelve to fifteen children as they came from other classes with their teacher to add to the work. They introduced them to the Lowry paintings, and told them what was now needed. They had already mixed paint for the newcomers, and had decided to lay down some basic rules. Large figures had to be painted at the bottom of the panel, and should be about the size of two thumbs. Small figures (about one thumb) should be near the houses at the top of the ground section. Of course there were exceptions, but these were accepted with good grace. The figures were painted directly with no preliminary drawing, but it was quite possible to paint them out and start again, or modify them if it proved necessary.

By the end of the second week every child in the school had played a part, together with all the members of staff, the school secretary, the caretaker, and a number of parents. It really was a whole school effort. Finally, the team came together again and assessed what had happened. There was much discussion, but they appeared well pleased. They felt the need now for what they saw to be finishing touches. Paint was mixed, and details added to people, buildings and backgrounds. A burglar appeared on a roof. It was finished at last, and everything was cleared away. The process was over, we had made our deadline, and the panel was duly packaged and sent to the showground. It returned to us some weeks later, having also been exhibited at Snape Maltings, much to the children's interest and pride. We gave it a place of honour at the end of a wide light corridor in the school, and it was here that it took on a new energy as children and adults talked about it, and took pleasure in pointing out their own particular piece.

We believe it to have been a valuable educational experience in which staff learned as well as the children. The planning, the designing, the modifying, the team work and language all played a part. We have no doubts of the value of children working with works of art. They really enjoyed it, and were well able to make connections between their own work and that of other artists.

The Lowry project painting

Looking at a Lowry painting

Girl, 4 years: after looking at a Lowry painting

THE PAINTBRUSH REPORT (p. 116)

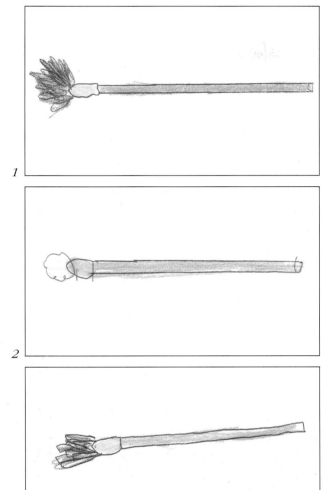

1

2

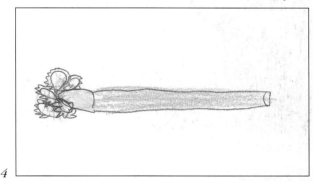

3

4

❛ 1 On Wednesday 18th November my table made paintbrushes out of dried flowers, wool, cotton and garden sticks. The first paintbrush was made with a garden stick, masking tape and tinsel. The tinsel was not very good. It would only take the first colour you used with it.

2 The second paintbrush I made was with cotton wool. It was quite good but on the third time I wet it, it fell in pieces.

3 My third paintbrush was made out of dried flower stems. They worked the best and they were strong.

4 My last paintbrush was made from daisies. They were good but petals flew all round my painting.

I enjoyed this activity. I liked painting the pictures. ❜

Louise. 8 years

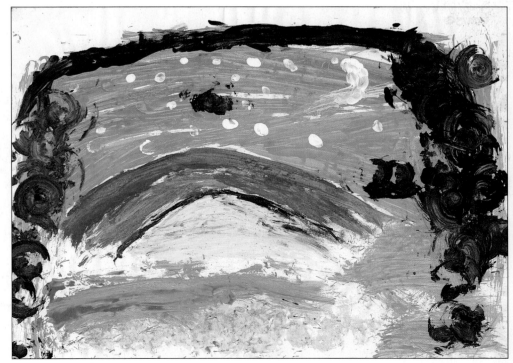

DESIGNING AND MAKING PAINTING TOOLS

A group of Year 2 BEd students were given the brief to design and make a set of painting tools. One of the students decided to take the brief and offer it to a group of eight-year-old children.

The children were asked to imagine that they had to paint a picture but that there were no conventional brushes available. They were supplied with thin garden canes for handles, a variety of materials from which to make the bristles, and masking tape to act as a ferrule joining the brush to the handle. The children were then asked to paint with their brushes and to write about them, describing them and evaluating their performance. To accompany the writing they also made a drawing of each brush, labelling the parts.

Value

This project is an art-related design activity which, as it investigates the appropriateness of materials for a particular purpose, is also closely related to technology. It encourages children to look for ways of making alternative mark-making tools and to enquire and to experiment.

Extension

The same challenge to experiment, design and find alternatives could be applied to many different tools, materials or designed forms. It could be of particular interest in relation to paint, with children investigating natural pigments such as earths, ochres and juices and evaluating their success for making pictures. This could be seen within an historical context, for example the investigation of cave paintings.

BUILDINGS
Printmaking

Middle School. Three classes. 11 and 12 years. 23 pupils.

Three separate classes from one year-group undertook projects based on the built environment. Two classes worked from direct experience, and the third from photographic resources.

1 Background

The children in this school work to a firmly structured developmental programme which includes two and three-dimensional art, textiles and design technology. We base a lot of the work on the experience of looking at art and design forms of all kinds - preferably originals. We also borrow art students' work from time to time.

A high proportion of the work is based on direct experience and the children are taught to gather resources and research for themselves continually. The use of sketchbooks is an integral part of this package. The whole purpose is to enable children to think creatively and imaginatively. This is supported on the one hand by experience and understanding of the elements of art, and on the other by techniques, which we teach structurally and sequentially following exploration and experimentation, by demonstration and discussion.

Each year all children will have looked at people, at natural form, at the environment, and at made forms. The challenges will differ, but the way I see it is that the child views them in a different light every year - it is really to do with the way in which they mature.

2 Class A and Class B: The Lavenham project

Lavenham (Suffolk) was chosen for a humanities project for its history as a Tudor wool town. Six classes (divided into sixteen groups) were accompanied by teachers for a full day's expedition. The group leader was responsible for working resources, including kits of drawing materials - pencils, pastels, and crayons. Work in school before the visit included historical background and a

Crooked house. On site drawing. 12 x 11.5 cm

Small house. On site drawing. 21.5 x 14 cm

video showing the methods of construction of timber framed houses.

Information-gathering was to be by means of writing, drawing, making notes and diagrams, and photography, and each child knew what to look for, and what was expected from them.

Art can be used to advantage on these occasions, and we are always careful that it does not degenerate into a poor servicing agent for other curriculum areas. It can service, but it is of so much more value when it is strong in its own right. The children knew they were to spend at least one hour working on a really good 'straight drawing', or drawings. This could be of a building, or a part of one. It was a good day, and we all enjoyed it.

Back in school the stimulus and research was followed up in cross-curricular humanities work; and in art, using the notes, diagrams, drawings and photographs, we moved into a printmaking project. In previous years the children had become familiar with monoprint, masking, found textures and block making. They had also worked into prints with graphic tools, paint and collage materials. This year lino printing was to be undertaken with some classes and Pressprint (polystyrene blocks) with the others. The subject seemed to lend itself particularly to these techniques.

Printmaking needs particular organisation in class layout, children's handling of tools and materials, and sensitivity to everyone else's needs if chaos is not to reign and resources be squandered.

In the first place each class undertook a period of general exploratory printmaking experience to consolidate what had been undertaken in the past, and before the introduction of the new techniques and materials. I believe this is a very important stage. The organisational rules are again underlined and rehearsed.

Following this the children gathered round and I introduced the lino with class A, and Pressprint with class B, also later with class C, who were working from different stimuli (see Tuscan Architecture project, page 120). I began by demonstrating a print from the uncut blocks, and asking them how they could be made more interesting. They soon understood that the lino could be cut away, and the Pressprint either indented by pressing found items into it, or by cutting. There were many suggestions, and much discussion ensued. I continued with the demonstration, using their ideas. Ideally they should be able to explore these materials for themselves, but I believe there are a few occasions when time and expense call for a different approach. I made a series of prints, working into the blocks at each stage. The lino prints were to be a straightforward positive/negative shape-based challenge, and the children in this class worked from their drawings, selecting appropriate information for a series of prints. The safe handling of cutting tools was carefully considered.

The Pressprint, which could not exceed the block size of 30 cms square, was to take the form of an 'elimination print'. This is a process where the minimally cut or unmarked block is first printed, before being further cut or indented prior to a second loading with ink. It is then printed directly on top (but not necessarily keyed exactly over the initial print). This procedure can be repeated, overlaying different colours, and carefully considering the effects as the elements interacted visually. The suggestion was that on this occasion they should work with light colours first, finishing with a dark one. The class returned to their drawings and researches and experimented with card viewfinders before finally making decisions about the composition of the print block. They were particularly involved in pattern and colour.

As this was a major project, all the children were printing, and eleven colour bases were organised in the room. These consisted of slabs (baking trays, or perspex), water colour inks which they mixed to desired colours, rollers, palette knives and newsprint. In each lesson, techniques and organisation were reinforced, and the children were taught specifically to put the ink in the corner,

The Swan. On site crayon drawing. 20 x 33

14.5 x 14 cm

Lino blocks. 29 x 29 cm

Pressprint on rolled ground. 29 x 31 cm

Pressprint (two processes). 32 x 32 cm

Pressprint (four processses). 29 x 28 cm

*Chalk and
pastel drawing.
50 x 16 cm*

*Pressprint.
29.5 x 16 cm*

*Chalk, pastel and charcoal
drawing. 62 x 15 cm*

*Pressprint.
35 x 16 cm*

Pressprint. 26 x 16 .5cm

*Pressprint.
35 x 14 cm*

*Pressprint.
37 x 17 cm*

*Pressprint. repeated on rolled
ground 33 x 34 cm*

but not too near the edge, of the slab, moving the required amount to the middle before rolling it and applying it to the blocks.

All the children were busy either printing, cutting and indenting, drawing and planning, or looking at other resource materials. Each child was encouraged to make three initial prints and to build them up in different ways, finally presenting one of them by means of a window mount. This added another display technique to their vocabulary. The work was presented, discussed and evaluated with emphasis on what had been learned, and how it could be used in other contexts.

Class C: The Tuscan Architecture project

Printmaking. Pressprint

We began in our usual manner of exploration and experimentation, using a variety of basic printing methods. The stimuli for this project consisted of second-hand images in the form of a series of colour photographs I had taken on a holiday in Italy. The subject matter was historic buildings, and my interests were strongly orientated towards colour, shape, light and shadow.

The children were grouped around the table, and we discussed the photographs and their content. Where did they think they had been taken? Was it in England? If not, how could they tell? What comparisons and differences could they see between this architecture, the light and shadow, and our own environment? What were these buildings made from? What were their functions?

Each child was given a long narrow piece of sugar paper (50 cms x 15 cms) and I invited them to study parts of their chosen photograph by means of a card viewfinder, and to choose a composition where shape and colour came together in what they considered to be a good design. They were then asked to make a pastel drawing before translating it into print. At this point I introduced them to the Pressprint, and demonstrated some of its potential, as in the previous projects.

The children were encouraged to ask themselves questions all the way through the working procedure, and to request assistance if they particularly needed it. I moved from group to group, and individual to individual, encouraging them and extending their thinking and practice, or drawing the attention of the whole class to relevant stages, or problems as they arose. I have always believed that a positive approach - drawing children's attention to the things which are working, and to the value of what they are doing - builds up confidence, and difficulties and so-called failures can then be seen in an appropriate context, faced, and overcome.

The method of working ran parallel to the Lavenham Pressprint project (see page 116) and each child selected and mounted a chosen print from their series, before presentation, discussion, assessment and evaluation.

Value

The value of these projects lies in their being seen as part of a continuum of research, practice and assessment. For me as a teacher, much of the assessment procedure is going on as I tutor individuals, although the children will not know it. Each project which requires research builds up the ability to do that very thing. Classroom practice consolidates and extends experience and requires selection and synthesis, in particular using the elements of line, shape, colour, tone, texture and pattern. The techniques of printmaking and presentation are extended. The self-assessment processes will require thought and encourage the children to see this particular work in the context of what has already happened and how it might be useful in the future.

Possible developments

Further research of other first hand experiences and secondary resources.

Developing ideas through print exploration and experiment.

Using print as a drawing technique, looking and directly interpreting, using found items etc, building up line, shape, colour.

Using printmaking and mixed media techniques in other ways and other contexts.

A practical study of patterning - textiles, wallpapers and furnishings.

A practical study of repeating unit patterns, natural and made.

A practical study of fine art prints, past and present.

A practical study of illustration and its communicative and expressive qualities.

Colour experience - working on themes of colour combinations, themes and moods.

Group work with the children building up images, either from individual units which are designed to fit together, or in large panels to fit in specific areas of the school or community.

Printing, leading to imprinting (into a substance like clay, or plasticine) and relief and textural work.

THE POPPY PROJECT

Primary school. Whole class (28 children). 9 - 11 years

1 Previous experience

The children in this school worked to a sequential developmental curriculum from entry. Within this structure staff and children were encouraged to work to their own ideas, enthusiasms and interests. In the early years experience was based on materials play, exploration and experimentation, with a balance of visual and imaginative challenges. Personal statement and expression was encouraged throughout, and children's imagery was respected. The diet of materials and tools included pencils, a variety of crayons, chalk, charcoal, home made bamboo pens, brushes, good quality powder and ready mixed colours, adhesives, clay, papier mâché, plaster, and a wide range of papers.

2 The work

At the other side of the school fence a field had been left to go wild before a supermarket was built on it. It lay on an upward incline, so from the school buildings it was in full view. Everybody was talking, because it was full of poppies which gradually opened until the full vista was a sea of scarlet which really did beckon us all to come and look - and do something about it.

On this particular day near the end of the summer term - when we were not really looking for new initiatives - the weather was wonderful, with a bright blue sky. The children could not stop looking out the windows, and asked if they could go out and draw and paint the poppies. They could enthuse me as much as I could them when it came to the point, so we went.

By road it would have been quite a long way, and since we had decided that we needed large drawing boards, paint, mixing palettes and water, as well as drawing tools, there were some problems to be considered.

The first decision we made was to comandeer the school wheelbarrow and load it with our needs. The second was to think of some means to get ourselves and all our equipment over the chain intermesh fence, as there was no gate on that side of the school. Much discussion ensued, and a number of ideas were put forward. The chosen plan of action was to build a strong bridge by means of lashing chairs together. The finishing touch was added in the form of a blanket which masked the upper edge of the wire. We made it, tested it very carefully, and put it to good use.

POPPIES

Poppies. Water colour. 25 x 35 cm

*Poppies. Pastel and crayon.
50 x 62 cm*

Misty poppies. Powder colour. 29 x 32 cm

Poppy painting with houses. 59 x 26 cm

Poppy. Pencil, ink and crayon.
9 x 19 cm

Sketch. Oil pastels and pencil.
14.5 x 22 cm

Poppies. Computer image.
15 x 16 cm

Poppy painting.
Powder colour.
46 x 59 cm

Poppy. Powder colour. 41 x 26 cm

Weaving on string warp. Rags, wool, lace
offcuts, cotton wool, fleece, paint. 54 x 39 cm

Having arrived in the field we (the children and two members of staff accompanying them) settled ourselves around the edge and just enjoyed the sheer experience of the place. When you were among the poppies you could see there were thousands of them, and they were of so many different hues - some in tight buds, and others at all stages of opening or seeding. They really were beautiful, very frail and silky. There was a surprising number of things growing among them - weeds and wild flowers of various kinds, and wheat from a past crop. We were aware of other kinds of life, too - insects, and birds flying up out of the growth.

This class always seemed to choose to dive into paint as their first response to any project, and this was no exception. The first visit allowed us only about half an hour of intense practical working. The children had been invited to sit in pairs, thus allowing for discussion, but undertaking individual work. At this stage most of them painted directly on to the paper and required little direction. They had been used to handling paint and were familiar with the challenge of 'showing what it looked, sounded, felt and smelled like' through their work. They enjoyed mixing colours - some were holding their loaded paint brushes against a poppy, or to the sky to see if they were satisfied with the match. Ears of wheat were picked and some children experimentally printed with them. By the end of the morning we had paintings, drawings, notes and found objects. Some children had begun two or three pieces of work.

The classroom had been prepared for the practical work. I believe that a classroom is a working room, and that from an early age children should be trained to keep it in working order, knowing where tools and materials are kept, and respecting their care and good usage. That does not mean that the room was always tidy - far from it! There must be strong organisation, and children must know the places they can or cannot work with the various tools and materials, which must be within easy reach.

For any project where a number of different things are happening children need organisational security, or chaos can ensue. There will be times when it will be necessary to make children aware of this organisation, and of one another's needs - but that is part and parcel of their education.

After lunch we went into the classroom and looked at what we had done, and at the collection of resources which I had introduced. These included large reproductions of Monet's 'Poppy fields', a variety of photographs, and wildflower books showing diagrams and pictures about poppies and what might be found in poppy fields. Language and science became important aspects in their own right, but never weakened or overtook the very powerful art statements or pushed them into becoming secondary illustrative matter.

On the second day we were back in the field for about an hour, enthusiasm still running high. This time the work really did take off, with the children following up their own ideas and collecting the information they knew they would need: cloud studies, poppy studies, landscape, the shapes, patterns and colours before them, relative sizes of shapes, words and characteristics. Some painted pictures, some made collections, or drew different aspects and sequences, or recorded information. One child made drawings of poppies at different stages - from bud to seed head, and another followed up by making drawings of poppies on the computer back in the classroom.

We returned to the field on two more occasions over the next few days. Each time was a new experience, and new work was undertaken, or more research material built up. In the classroom the children were working on or from the out-of-door studies and collections - all the research was coming together and being selected, developed and used.

The work was wide-ranging in scale and nature. There were paintings, collages, drawings, constructions, repeating patterns, textiles, weaving, and clay models, in sequences or single forms. There were small delicate line drawings and paintings, and quite large pieces which covered two or three pieces of sugar or cartridge paper stuck together. Some wrote, and descriptive vocabulary built up: 'field of the finest silk', 'the petals of butterfly wings', 'the inside - of milk', 'nodding their sleepy heads', 'the most beautiful poppy field ever'.

What was so pleasing was the way the children persevered when they came up against difficulties, technical problems, or things that they were not satisfied with. One piece of work which exemplified this but which sadly was not recorded was the work of a nine-year-old girl. This child looked at her painting, a large poppy head on a long stalk. 'I'd love to make a huge one,' she said, pointing two metres up from the ground. She proceeded to collect the necessary bits from the classroom resource bank. Soon she had made the centre seedhead from fabric, sewn and stuffed solid. She outlined the petals with wire and stretched thin material over it. She was pleased, but thought long and hard about the problem of the stem. Wire was a good base but looked too thin, so she bound cotton wool around it with thongs of fabric. 'It doesn't look like a poppy stalk,' she said. 'It's not hairy.' A further sortie to the bit box led to the discovery of some coarse green wool, which she wrapped around the whole length. The texture was changed but she was still not satisfied. 'The hairs don't stick out,' she said, deep in thought. She was next seen teasing out ends of wool so that it really was hairy. 'It's better, but it's not right - they are green, not silvery green.' The finishing touch, after discussion, was added by using silver spray, very carefully masking the areas she wanted to leave green. 'It's terrific!' she said when finally appraising the effect. It measured over two metres high, and one metre in diameter.

It was very interesting to see parents making their way into the classroom at the end of each day to see what had been going on, and becoming very involved in what was happening. The poppies had moved them too.

Besides the interest in art and design, involving children in researching, exploring, experimenting and in using the elements of line, pattern, tone, colour, texture, form and space, our interests were also cross-curricular, with science, language and technology playing very strong roles which have only been touched on here. You could say that our bridge was an interesting problem-solving challenge too - a self-imposed design brief because we had found a real need! It worked very well.

We celebrated the whole project by putting up an exhibition around the school and in the classroom. The project really had caused a lot of interest. It was at this point that the term came to an end.

3 Value

This project seems to have been one of those events where the whole ethos for learning, approaches and skills which had been fostered in the classroom, came together with an opportunity to use subject matter which clearly engendered enthusiasm and creative energy. It is a good example for making the point that a defined curriculum only lays down the content of the learning, and not the vehicle by which is undertaken. It would be hard to believe that this experience could have been missed because the teacher had a different piece of subject matter written in for that particular time.

The whole list of activities subsumed under the headings of *Investigating and making, Knowing and understanding* (Key Stage 1, see page 18) are clearly present, together with Key Stage 2 skills of *communicating ideas and feelings, developing ideas or themes, experimenting with and applying knowledge of the elements of art, planning and making, choosing appropriate media, adapting and modifying*, and *discussing*. The introduction of the Monet painting, the photographs and diagrams are part of a wider programme in regard to *identifying different kinds of art and design* and *looking for purposes*. Children were encouraged and taught to think for themselves and to use their own initiative.

DRAWING FROM DIRECT EXPERIENCE

All the drawings on this page are from resources which have been introduced into the classroom. The teachers have challenged children of different age groups to look intently and to respond, supporting them by means of appropriate media, choice of tools, and by tutorial and stimulating involvement.

The barn owls were live residents of a sanctuary, who could not for various reasons be returned to the wild. It is interesting to note the approaches of children at different stages of development to the same kind of stimuli and introduction. Both responses are valid.

Mushroom. Sugar paper collage.
10 years. 19 x 20 cm

Narcissus. Powder on black sugar
paper. 9 years. 23.5 x 11.5 cm

Still life. Charcoal and pastel.
Boy, 10 years.
53 x 35.5 cm

Barn owl.
Crayon and felt tip.
Boy, 5 years.
26.5 x 20 cm

Barn owl. Chalk and pastel on black
sugar paper. Boy, 8 years.
33 x 27 cm

126

RESEARCH AND SEQUENCING

High School. Girl, 12 years

In order to consolidate and extend children's ability to research and develop ideas, in their first years in this secondary school sketchbook work and sequencing are specifically taught and encouraged continually. It is a fundamental need for their current and future work. To begin with, children undertake intense 'looking' experience, using natural stimuli, which for this particular project included shells, bones and plant forms. This leads on to thinking about shape, pattern and composition, and finally takes the potential of colour into consideration, together with the appropriate vocabulary. The first colour experience is based on the scheme of a painting chosen for particular qualities by the child. The experience is basically practical, but is supported throughout by the teacher's encouragement to the child to communicate what he or she is thinking - in spoken or written form.

Self assessment must always be an integral part of the practical and thinking process. This is what makes it so valuable.

Research and developments using graphic tools and watercolour

❝ I found a painting that was brightly coloured and all the colours complemented each other, so I decided to use it. It had both light and dark blues and bright pinks and greens along with purple and beige, a touch of lilac and a dirty yellow. On my bigger painting I decided to change the mood of the colours to harmonising greens and blues and some soft yellows. I did the patchy type of painting because I thought it made it look more interesting. ❞

Joanna Matthews

Art Advisers Association	*Learning Through Drawing*	AAA North Eastern Region 1978
Bono, Edward de	*Lateral Thinking: a textbook of creativity*	Penguin, 1977
Curriculum Council for Wales	*Art in the National Curriculum. Non Statutory Guidance for Teachers*	CCW 1992
Department for Education	*Art in the National Curriculum [England]*	HMSO 1992
Department for Education	*Art in the National Curriculum [Wales]*	HMSO 1992
Donaldson, Margaret	*Children's Minds*	Faber/Collins 1978
Dyson, Anthony [Editor]	*Looking, making, learning,* The Bedford Way Series	Kogan Page, 1989
Edwards, Betty	*Drawing on the right side of the brain*	Souvenir Press, 1981
Field, Dick	*Change in art education*	Routledge & Kegan Paul, 1970
Fulton, John	*Materials in design and technology*	Design Council, 1992
Gardner, Howard	*Artful scribbles*	Jill Norman, 1980
Gentle, Keith	*Children and art teaching*	Croom Helm, 1985
Goodnow, Jacqueline	*Children's drawings*	Fontana/Open Books, 1977
Hoffnung, Annetta	*Hoffnung*	Gordon Fraser, 1988
Jameson, Kenneth & Kidd, P	*Pre-school play*	Studio, 1974
Jackson, Margaret	*Display and environment*	Hodder & Stoughton, 1993
Joicey, H B	*An eye on the environment: an art education project*	Unwin Hyman, 1988
Kellogg, Rhoda	*Analysing children's art*	California, 1972
Mathieson, Kevin	*Children's art and the computer*	Hodder & Stoughton, 1993
Morgan, Margaret (editor)	*Art 4 - 11*	Blackwell, 1988; Simon & Schuster, 1992
Morris, Desmond	*The biology of art*	Methuen, 1962
National Curriculum Council	*Art: non statutory guidance (England)*	NCC, 1992
Newland, Mary & Rubens, Maurice	*Some functions of art in the primary school*	ILEA Teachers Art Centre, 1984
Nicholson, Winifred	*Unknown colour*	Faber, 1987
Paine, Sheila (editor)	*Six children draw*	Academic Press, 1981
Robertson, Seonaid Mairi	*Rose garden and labyrinth*	Routledge, 1963
Robertson, Seonaid Mairi	*Creative crafts in education*	Routledge & Kegan Paul, 1952
Sedgwick, Fred and Dawn	*Drawing to learn*	Hodder & Stoughton, 1993
Taylor, Rod	*Educating for art*	Longman, 1986